INSIDE OF ME

Wendy Shipman

Copyright © 2018 Wendy Shipman

All rights reserved. This book or any portion thereof may not be reproduced or transmitted in any form or by any means, including photocopying, recording, taping or by any information storage or retrieval system without the express written consent of the author.

The names, characters, places or incidences in this book are strictly fictional and the product of the author's imagination. Any resemblance to actual people, living or dead, is entirely coincidental.

Scripture notation taken from the Amplified Bible, YouVersion Bible App, 2018.

ISBN-13: 978-0-578-41763-9

DEDICATION

Betty Oldham

You have always believed in me when I didn't believe in myself. And for that alone, I will love you for the rest of my life.

ACKNOWLEDGEMENTS

God… I thank You first and foremost. You created in me a gift I knew I had, but never thought I was good enough. Thank you for proving me wrong.

My gratitude goes beyond just adding names to this book. So many people have blessed me in one way or another when God allowed our paths to cross. I sincerely thank you.

To my mother **Wilhelmena Poinsette** and my father the late **Ezekiel Poinsette**, thank you for giving me the gift of life. I love you.

To my husband **Russell Shipman, Sr.**, thank you for your unconditional love, honesty and support throughout this process. You were there to give me that extra push I needed to keep going. My love, you never doubted my abilities to be great. You are my life, my heart, my love - my ALWAYS. I love you!

To my three children Alexis, Rodney Jr., and Russell Jr., thank you for inspiring me to be a great mother. And my prayer is to strive to be an inspiration to all of you. **Alexis Oldham**, you were (are) my shining light when I saw nothing but darkness. **Rodney Oldham, Jr.**, you were (are) the air I breathed when I was suffocating. **Russell Shipman, Jr.**, God blessed me the opportunity to love another child as my own. I love you all - FOREVER.

To all of my family and friends back home in Summerville, South Carolina and my new family in Birmingham, Alabama, I love you.

Thank you for all the ones who said YES, but God said NO.
* Yes, you read that right. *
If it wasn't for you, this really would not be possible.

Cover Design: SelfPubBookCovers.com/BravoCovers

Formatting by: ebooklaunch.com

Photographer: Mr. Meredith White, Birmingham, AL

Hairstylist: Ms. Jennifer Anthony, PROtective Styles by Jenn

PREFACE

Surviving depression is not as easy as some may seem. Speaking from experience, there were times when I found myself inside of a deep, dark bottomless hole; all the while smiling like nothing was wrong. However, on the days where I could manage to lift a pen, I began to write. Writing my feelings on paper was like a release of the pain that was INSIDE OF ME.

So many people suffer with depression like I do. This book is meant to inspire those that feel like you can't survive… but you can! You can free yourself from the depths of despair by seeking therapy, support from family/friends, medication and/or counseling.

YOU are significant and YOU do matter! Always remember that!

CHAPTER ONE

"Saints turn your bibles to the Book of Matthew, chapter ten, verses twenty-six through twenty-eight. Amen?" as Pastor Benson looks over his glasses, making sure he had the full attention of his members.

"Amen!" rang out the congregation as they stood at their seats.

"Amen," I said as I flipped through the pages of my bible. I really and truly want to be completely here, but my spirit and my mind are elsewhere. *Judean, if you can just make it through service, I thought to myself, you promised Annette you would get out of the house and find refuge and peace at church.* Not sure about finding anything today, but at least I made it.

"Follow along, if you will, for the reading of God's Word." I can see the Pastor shifting his glasses to accommodate his failing eyes. For some strange reason, it seemed like for ten seconds, his eyes were fixed me. Almost as if he was giving me a forewarning - This verse is for you, Judean.

As Pastor Benson spoke, the church reverberated with a great abundance… like God himself was speaking. **"So,** *do not be afraid of them, for nothing is hidden that will not be revealed, or kept secret that will not be made known."*

"Yes, Lord!" some parishioners shouted.

"... What I say to you in the dark, tell it in the light; and what you hear whispered in your ear, proclaim from the housetops."

"Preach, Pastor!" "Hallelujah!"

"... Do not be afraid of those who kill the body but cannot kill the soul, but rather be afraid of Him who can destroy both soul and body in hell. And let all of God's people say, Amen."

"Amen!" bellowed the church members.

"Yes, God! Say so, Pastor!" Sista Patrice yelled, waving her hand and showing all thirty-two of her teeth.

If she don't be quiet and have several seats, I thought to myself. Sigh. Everybody knows she has a 'thing' for the Pastor. It can't get any more obvious. If Pastor doesn't acknowledge her soon, I swear one day she is going to come to church naked, in heels, still showing all thirty-two. Pastor Benson is bound to notice her then, shaking my head to myself.

Pastor Benson announced, "The subject for today is *You can run, but you can't hide*. You all may be seated."

Hand claps and amens were echoing throughout the church building. And what a beautiful building it is. I had been worshiping here for several years. Elijah, well, he came to church every now and then. Work kept him busy. This church is like home to me. The members were very helpful during the passing of my husband. You have your ones who only help to be nosy. But for the most part, most of them were very sincere.

As Pastor began to preach, I began to fade into another world. My world. My life with my husband of twenty-three years always seems to creep back into my mind when I should be focusing on other things. You would think after a few months of his departure on earth, it would be easier. But far from it. Elijah was my everything. We spent the first few years loving ourselves and each other before we planned on Elijah, Jr. Our marriage was not perfect by any means. We had our ups and downs like any married couple would. All in all, I believed in our vows, told God before our family and friends that we would be man and wife till death. I can honestly say, I believed God gave me my soul mate. I was happy. We were able to buy a house together, raise a son who was now away at college and happily on our way to retirement. Although sometimes, I wondered if he was happy with me. Often, Elijah would be so distant, like I was bothering him. I just assumed it was mid-life crisis. But I still loved him. Therefore, I can't understand why God took him away from me. He wasn't supposed to have a heart attack and die, not the man I loved with all my being. Noooooo, God! Not now! Elijah was my life; the very air I breathe. I don't want to live without him.

"Are you alright, honey?" a woman whispered and gave me a Kleenex just as the second tear drop rolled down my cheek. I didn't realize my eyes were welled up with tears much less falling.

"Yes, ma'am." I was able to assemble a small fraction of a smile as I blotted my cheeks. "Thank you."

The pastor was still preaching. I am oblivious to anything going on around me. Not even noticing the innocent stare from the little girl in front of me as she holds on tightly to her Daddy's neck. She was looking at me with those big, beautiful brown eyes. Almost as if she was looking into my hurt soul.

"I don't know about you, Saints, but I'm glad to be here… I'm glad to be among the land of the living … and rejoicing! God didn't have to do it, but He did!" Pastor Benson exclaimed.

"Gloooo-rayyyy!" "Praise God!" "Jesus!" yelled the people of God.

Half the congregation was standing and agreeing with the Pastor's message. Sista Patrice is doing her usual agreement with Pastor. Jumping up and down so much that her breasts were about to shout right out of her dress. It's a wonder that Pastor can still concentrate on his sermon while Sista's triple DDDs are catching the eyes of every Deacon on the side wall.

She needs to sit her fast tail down, I thought to myself. Realizing what I was thinking, I looked around to make sure I didn't say it out loud. I looked up and the little girl in front of me was smiling with her pacifier in her mouth. I smiled back. I think she heard my spirit and it tickled her, too.

Once Pastor preached the Word, anyone who was willing and able could go to the altar for prayer. I could always use some. I walked up front and knelt at the altar. Pastor placed his hand on my head and asked God to give me peace in my time of sorrow. The warmth that I felt go through my body, I knew it was God's anointing. At that moment, I felt like God was going to change something in my life, but I didn't know what. As I got up after Pastor prayed, instead of walking back to my seat, I exited the building. Today, I don't want to talk to anyone. I am not ready for the questions. "How are you doing?" "Do you need anything?" "Are you making it without Elijah?" "Can I do anything for you?" Sigh… I just can't deal with that today. I did my part. I showed up as promised.

On my way to the house, I stopped by the grocery store. As I sat in the car, I thought about what to fix for dinner. My men will be hungry when I get home. Suddenly, my heart stopped beating for what seemed like minutes … was only two seconds. Reality set in… no one is at the house. No one will be there to fix dinner for. No one there to hear me talk about Sunday service. No one there to hear how the little girl and I laughed at me thinking bad thoughts about Sista Patrice. Suddenly, the blood in my body froze. I felt ice cold. My heart felt like it was going to beat right out of my chest cavity. I can hear my heartbeat in the arteries in my neck. The air was stifling, and I can't breathe. I'm afraid to put down the window. Fear has taken over my body. I can't move.

"Oh, God!" I murmured as I grabbed my chest. I am having a heart attack. *Am I going to die in my car? Will someone walking to their car find me in time to get me to the hospital?* Then, for a split second, I thought … *but if I die, maybe I will see Elijah again*. Elijah. Maybe it is my time to be with my husband again. I smiled. Just the thought of seeing him once again made me shudder. But I can't leave my son. He still needs one of his parents and I am the only one left.

The parking lot seemed like a black and white swirl of light that I can't stop from spinning. "Jesus, please help me." I closed my eyes and said a prayer. "Yea, though I walk through the valley of the shadow of death, I will fear no evil, for Thou art with me." I kept repeating those words until I could feel the blood warming up my cold skin. I can breathe once again. Inhale… exhale. *You can do this, Judean*, I thought to myself. Everything is getting clearer and brighter. Finally, I can focus enough to reach for the handkerchief in my purse. I patted my forehead and behind my neck.

My cell phone rang.

Inhaling deeply as I gasped for air. "Hello?"

"Hey, Ma! How are you?"

"I'm fine, son. How are you?" trying to muster a smile behind my answer.

"I'm great! Why do you sound like you are out of breath? Were you exercising?"

"Exercising? Ha… no baby. I was just loading grocery bags into the car."

I lied so EJ wouldn't know about my anxiety attack. I downed the window to catch a small breeze so I can breathe a little better and so he could hear the outside noise on the other end. Some things I don't like to share with him. Although he is grown enough to know, he has his own life to deal with. And I really don't know how he would react knowing that his mother suffers from anxiety.

"Oh, okay. Momma, I just wanted you to know I'm on my way home."

"Home? Why?"

"Why? You don't want to see me?" EJ sneered.

"Oh… no…" as I chuckled. "Of course, I would love to see you, baby. I just didn't expect it, that's all."

"Okay then. I'll be there in about an hour and a half."

"Great!" A sense of relief comes over me. I won't be alone in that quiet house tonight. "I'll make you something to eat. Any suggestions, my child?" I asked playfully.

"Ma, anything you cook is fine with me. I love you, beautiful lady. See you soon."

I get so warm, almost blushing, when my son calls me 'beautiful'. I know he only calls me beautiful because I am his mother. Either way, just those kind words makes me think - maybe I am beautiful.

"I love you, my handsome son. See you later, baby."

"Ok, Ma. Later." Then silence.

"Alright Judean, get yourself together." I murmured to myself. "You need to get some groceries to make dinner. EJ is coming home."

CHAPTER TWO

Shuffling around in the kitchen, I realized it was too late to start a full Sunday dinner. I'll just keep it simple - grilled NY strip steak and caramelized onions, sautéed asparagus in garlic butter topped with bacon bits, and Old Bay roasted potatoes. Simple, yet filling.

Sunday afternoons, at one time, were memorable in this house. EJ would bring some of his friends over after church to watch sports on T.V. Just hearing their voices brought life into this otherwise quiet house. Cheering for their favorite opposing teams was like literally being in the stands. Such competitiveness made me giggle every time they got together. Elijah, however, would spend most of his time in his study with the door closed or outside on the patio looking at the Sunday newspaper - if it was one of his weekends home. If it wasn't for the boys, I would feel lonely in my own house. But at least I wasn't alone.

I heard a car door slam and raced to the front door. Coming up the walkway was my baby. A good-looking young man who was tall in stature - the making of a GQ male model. Where did the years go? He was just an infant I was holding in my arms. I looked at my son and can't believe how strong and attractive he has become. My heart swells with pride.

As EJ came to meet me with his arms outstretched, his smile glistens in the sun. "Hey, Mom!"

"Hello EJ!" as I looked up to my son. "Are you going to stop getting taller?" I asked.

We both held on to each other for a few moments. *Thank you, God, for blessing me with this child*, I murmured under my breath. "How was the drive?" I asked.

"Not bad at all. I spent most of my time talking to LaTika. Or I should say, she spent most of my time talking to me," as he stares off for a few seconds - smiling.

"LaTika? I never heard you mention her before," giving him a side-eye.

"Ehhhh, I've only dated her for a few weeks. She is a very nice young lady… very respectable. I believe she would be someone that you would like. I'll invite her to come with me the next time I drive home."

"That's great, honey. You seem happy. And that is what matters when it comes to being with someone. Happiness."

"Yeah… well for me, I expect much more than just happiness in a relationship, Mom. And speaking of happiness," EJ's hand motioned me towards the door, "let's go inside."

***

"Dinner was great, Momma. Thank you."

"No need to thank me, son. It was my pleasure. You are a pleasant surprise to my day. Honestly, I was dreading coming home after church." My eyes shifted to the corner of the dining room. It doesn't take much for tears to form in my eyes.

"Oh, you made it to church today? That's good to hear. You haven't been very social since dad died."

"Well, to tell you the truth, I was never really that social when he was alive."

"That's true, Ma. But you seemed to be a little more outgoing at one point. It was good to see you going shopping and on lunch dates with Auntie Annette. How is she, by the way?"

"She's good. She is the one who made me promise to get out of the house today." I snickered. "If anything, church was very entertaining."

EJ curled his lips and tilted his head to the side. "Don't tell me. Was Ms. Patrice *'shaking-what-her-momma-gave-her'* this morning?"

We both laughed so hard we were holding our stomachs.

"Ma, I've never met her, but the stories you tell are hilarious."

"She's fairly new to our church. She started attending after you left for college. I really don't know her that well. But what little I do know, she is looking for a husband. THAT is obvious!"

EJ and I laugh for a few more minutes and then I proceeded to get up to clear the table. But EJ grabbed my arm as I stood up.

"Momma, there is a reason I came home to see you. I wanted to talk to you about some things that are on my mind. I figured it was better to talk to you in person versus over the phone. Can we go into the living room to talk? I can help you with the dishes later."

"Sure baby." I could see the concern on his face. As I walked to the couch in the living room, I began to shake. I'm beginning to feel anxious even though I have no idea what EJ wanted to talk about. "Oh Lord." I whispered.

"First of all, Mom, there is nothing wrong with me... I promise."

A sigh of relief must have shown on my face because EJ patted my hand as he sat down beside me.

"I figured you automatically would have thought something was wrong with me. There isn't. I'm still that healthy, handsome son of yours." smiled EJ as he winked at me.

"Yes, my healthy, handsome son. Thank God for that! So, what's wrong, EJ?"

"Mom, I am here because I am concerned about you."

"Me?" taken aback by his candor.

"Yes, you."

"Son, I am fine. I mean, it does get lonely sometimes. But I am fine. Besides, you have school ... a-a-and work...

a-a-and LaTika to think about instead of me. You don't worry about your old Momma." I managed to smile, forcing myself not to start tearing up.

"Ma… stop! Stop! You are MY priority." EJ said sternly. "You, always have been, always will be. You are the one who made me the man that I am. Not dad… YOU. So yes, I will always be concerned about my girl."

This time, I couldn't hold back that tear. It slipped out of the corner so fast, I couldn't catch it. So, I just let it fall freely.

"Mom, I am really concerned about your health. I know for the most part you are pretty healthy physically for your age. However, I am not completely naive to your mental state."

I gazed at EJ wide-eyed in disbelief. I never really knew how observant he was of me.

"Dad's death has taken a toll on me. So, I know it must have been really tough for you. I know you want to portray to me how strong you are, but I know you are hurting. And I know you are depressed. Mom, in all honesty, you have been depressed for as long as I can remember."

"What? EJ, what are you…"

EJ interrupted, "Mom, I'm not the 10-year-old child that you tell to 'go to your room' or say 'you don't know what you are talking about' anymore. I'm a grown man and I can see that my mother is depressed. Dealing with Dad,

I'm surprised you never committed yourself to a mental hospital."

At that moment, I saw anger in EJ's eyes I had never seen before. That wrinkle in the middle of his forehead always meant he was mad about something. But to hear him talk about his dad in that manner really floored me. I never thought that EJ would see his father as 'the bad guy'. It seems I underestimated my son. Then curiosity got the best of me. I wondered what else EJ was feeling.

CHAPTER THREE

"EJ, I have to admit. I am at a loss for words by your statement. Why would you say that you are surprised I haven't committed myself?"

"Mom, I am about to say this as respectfully as I know how."

"You know I've always told you to never hold things internally. Say what's on your mind."

EJ looked directly into my eyes and said, "Dad was a narcissistic, egotistical bully. And that is the nice version of what I am really thinking."

"EJ!" as I look at my son flabbergasted.

"No... no... Ma, listen." EJ stood up. He walked to the mantle and stared at our family picture. After gazing for a moment, he resumed talking. "I respect the man because he was my father. But that's all. He was not the sharpest knife in the drawer. I saw the way he treated you and the way he belittled you. As a child, what could I do? You always taught me to be obedient towards you and dad. I was always respectful and never talked back. However," EJ pointed his finger in the air to catch my attention, "it would have been another story altogether if he had put his hands on you." EJ rubbed his hand over his right knuckle as he talked. "He wasn't completely crazy. That's what made me realize that Dad was all tongue and teeth. He would only hurt you with words. I do think he succeeded at times to make you feel unworthy. The way you handled yourself, though, was remarkable in that it 'looked' like it didn't faze you. Now that I am older, I can see that it did. You were just able to hide the hurt internally. Sometimes verbal abuse can be worse than being physically abused."

"Son, I am stunned by your perception of your father. And I really don't want to discuss his transgressions with you. However, your observation about Elijah is correct. He was mean and hateful. But I made a vow to God for better and for worse. And I never backed down on any promises I made to God."

"I'm sure God didn't want you to be a fool either." Realizing what he said, EJ sat back down next to me. "Look Ma, Dad is gone. He is never coming back. He will not walk back in that door and chastise you for talking bad about him to me. His transgressions have made your life hell. I know… I was there, remember? Whatever things dad said to you to make you feel less than deserving was wrong. And you shouldn't carry that burden the rest of your life. You don't have to shelter yourself anymore. You need to enjoy life. Enjoy the world while you are still able."

For a hot moment, I felt like Pastor Benson was looking through my son's eyes. It was the same look I sensed when I was in church this morning. Like God was looking into my eyes and embracing my tattered soul. It scares me because what if God could really see what my soul looks like. I mean, I know God is omnipotent and He sees all… but I don't want Him to know just how empty I am inside. It's selfish and almost embarrassing because I have been blessed beyond what I could have imagined. I love the Lord. However, I also hurt in the inside. How can I love God, but I don't love what's in the inside of me?

"Ma!"

I jumped.

"Are you all right? You zoned out on me."

"Yes, I'm good. I was just thinking."

"About?"

"Well son, to be honest with you, your father was not the only person in my life that has let me down." Before I knew it, I realized I spoke too much. I didn't mean to say it. Or maybe I did. It was, however, like a small sense of relief to share some of my pain. But not with my only child, Lord. I'm supposed to listen to him and give HIM advice. Not the other way around. Just then Pastor Benson's voice echoed in my ear, *"You can run, but you can't hide."*

"What do you mean, Ma? Talk to me, please."

As I look at the hurt in my son's eyes, the tears begin to well in mine. I looked down, just so I didn't have to see the disappointment in his face. At that point, I did want to run. I needed to escape my reality. I wanted to crawl into my bed, bury my head underneath my comforter and just sleep it away. But I am here having a meltdown in front of my own child.

Still gazing at the floor, I squeezed EJ's hands and said, "Son, outside of you, my life has been nothing but hurt, heartaches, and disappointments. I can honestly say my life had no meaning until I had you. You were the beat of my heart. It was you who kept me going. Otherwise, I would have…" I looked up at my son. I will not complete my last statement. The devil will not make me say what I want to say. Not that. Not to EJ.

"Baby, I am going to go into the kitchen and make us some coffee. Then we can sit down and have a very candid conversation about your Mom's life. Are you okay with that?"

"Of course, Momma. I'll wait for you right here until you get back. I'm not going anywhere." EJ reached over and kissed my forehead.

CHAPTER FOUR

I brought a tray from the kitchen with coffee mugs, coffee, spoons and French Vanilla creamer. EJ was never fond of coffee until he found flavored creamers. Now he can't go a day without drinking coffee. Maybe that's because the college life required that extra caffeine for midnight studying.

EJ walked over to grab the tray from my hands. "Ma, you should have called me. I would have helped you."

"Baby, when you are used to doing things by yourself, it becomes a habit. No big deal."

"Well, when I am here, you call on me. Mom, you are a Queen. You are worthy of being waited on hand and foot. You just never got to understand that by being around Dad."

There is that forehead wrinkle again. EJ walked to the coffee table and placed the tray down. He waited for me to sit down before he took a seat next to me on the couch.

I smiled at EJ. I thank God I did raise him to be everything NOT like his father. "Thank you, son."

As I reached for the coffee mug, I saw 'the look' from EJ. So, I sat back on the couch, pulled my hands back and waited for my son to pour me some coffee. As we both got settled and found comfort on the couch, I began to say a silent prayer of understanding. I took the mug from EJ and wrapped both hands around it. The warmth of it gave me some sense of comfort. I sipped my coffee and my thoughts began to drift to my childhood. The thought of it made my insides burn like acid. I never wanted to go back there. Ever. But, since my son wanted to talk, here we are. Sigh.

"Son, I never talked about my childhood because it was a never a pleasant place for me. It was a dark time in my life where I felt like I didn't belong here. Honestly, a place where I didn't want to be. My Mother, your grandmother Carolyn, made it quite obvious that I was not a 'plan' in her life. I was never good enough. I was never as beautiful as my sister Marjorie. I was never considered a daughter to love. I was just a daughter because she gave birth to me."

"Momma, that can't be how Grandma Carolyn felt?"

"You've never been around your grandmother long enough to really tell. I kept you away from all of that negativity as much as possible. That's why your Dad and I chose to move away from home. Well… I should say your Dad more than myself. But that was fine with me because there was nothing in my hometown for me anyway."

EJ looked puzzled. "Why did Dad want to move?"

"Honestly, I don't know. I never asked him why he chose this place. But because he was my husband, I went with him."

Thinking back, that was a question I did ask at one time, but Elijah never did respond. So, I never asked again.

"As I was saying, growing up was not a pleasant time for me. I was always yelled at for the things I did… things I didn't do. I even got chastised for the things my sister did. If she did something bad, it was my fault for 'making' her do it. In my mother's eyes, Marjorie could never do any wrong. My mother never wanted me, EJ. You could tell just by her actions." I paused and inhaled deeply. "I also heard it." I felt my spirit escape from my body. I closed my eyes and imagined me standing behind my 10-year-old self and gazing at my mother and grandmother.

"Wait, you heard it? She told you this?" EJ voice seemed to echo while my mind travels back in time.

"She told me indirectly by the way she treated me. But I actually heard it one night when I was about 10 years old. I couldn't sleep so I got up to get a drink of water from the kitchen. I heard Momma talking to my grandmother, your great-grandmother, Thelma Jean.

***

"Carolyn, what is wrong witcha, child? Judean is ya own flesh and blood. Why is ya so mean to that girl? Ya think she don't see how ya love up on Marjee but ya don't love up on her?"

"Mother, you know I didn't want this child. She brings back too many bad memories of her daddy."

"Well, you's the one who opened ya legs for 'em."

"Mother... really?" Carolyn got up and walked over to the kitchen window to avoid Momma Jean's eyes. Those eyes could pierce right through your soul.

"Yeah... really! It ain't Judean's fault how she was conceived. You and her daddy made that baby. Don't you treat that child like she is some demon. She is a blessin' from tha Lawd. She is a blessin' from yo, sin." Momma Jean pointed her finger at my Momma.

Carolyn turned around and said, "I wouldn't even have her now, but you made me keep her. Otherwise, I would have given her up. And if I did, we wouldn't be having this conversation, would we Mother?" That sarcastic mouth my Momma used made Momma Jean even madder.

"And I's still stand by that. You's so uppity you can't even see what a blessin' that child is. But one day, ya will see which child will do fa ya when times get bad. Mark my words, child. As God is my witness, ye shall see."

***

"As a child, you can't imagine the hurt I felt knowing that your own Momma didn't want you. And would have gotten rid of you if someone didn't intervene. That night changed my life. I went back to my room and wept like someone close to me died. Actually, someone did die. Me. My soul was shattered like broken glass. And to be quite honest with you, EJ, as long as I have been alive, those shattered pieced have never been fixed. Not even your dad was able to fix them."

I was unaware that EJ had gotten up off of the couch until I felt him place a tissue from the box into my hand. When I looked up at him standing over me, I realized how wet my face was with tears.

"Thank you, baby." I wiped my eyes, but the tears kept flowing.

EJ could see the hurt in my eyes. He has never seen me like this before. I am always the strong woman he's grown up to know and love. That's how I wanted him to see his mother. Not some crybaby or defeated woman.

"Ma, I am at a loss of words" as he rubbed his neck in disbelief. "I would have never thought those words would have come out of Grandma Carolyn's mouth. But like you said, we were never around much so I would not have noticed."

"The memories of not being loved are forever etched in my spirit. After I heard those words, I changed. I lost my childhood. I had no more life in me … so it seemed at the time. I mean, how can I forget that, EJ? How can I just forget that my own mother didn't want me? She didn't want me at all."

I grabbed my mug and drank some more coffee. It's not as warm and comforting as it once was. It's just like my mind right now… lukewarm but on the way of being cold and unpleasant.

CHAPTER FIVE

I reached over and pour a little more coffee into my mug to warm up my already cooled portion. I had no need for creamer or sugar this time. I had no desire to taste anything. I just wanted to quench my dry throat. EJ is looking at me, patiently waiting on the next words to come out of my mouth.

"My sister Marjorie was always the 'beautiful one' in my mother's eyes. She was always entering her into beauty contests and talent shows. It is because Momma always knew her dearest daughter would become something one day. Marjorie was the prime example of a 'daughter that could do no wrong'. She was beautiful, very intelligent and played the piano. Momma Carolyn would spend every dime she had to make sure that Marjorie had everything she needed. The best clothes and shoes, weekly piano lessons, membership dues paid to all of the 'smart kids clubs' in high school. I couldn't even join a club because we didn't have enough money to spare. Imagine that." I said sarcastically. "I mean really? It's what I should have expected being the unloved child and all?" Even I smirked at my sarcasm. EJ was emotionless as he stared at me.

"I'll never forget the time my sister and I had this one on one conversation when we were teenagers. I was watching her get dressed for a date with Floyd, the cutest boy who played varsity basketball. Even though he had a reputation for being with a lot of girls back then, my sister was so excited."

***

"Marjorie, you do know that your date is a lady's man, right? I mean he is known for hurting girls' hearts after playing with them."

"Judean, you sound jealous," as she looked at me backwards in the mirror.

"Jealous? Are you kidding me? I don't find him the least bit attractive."

"Trust me when I say he doesn't find you attractive either."

Looking at my sister as she took off the pullover sweater and reached for the buttoned-down sweater I asked, "How do you know?"

Marjorie flipped her long, pressed hair from underneath the sweater and pivoted back in forth in the mirror to glance at herself from all angles.

"Oh, we were discussing classmates and I told him you were my sister. He was so shocked to know that we were siblings because... well .... he said there was no way we were sisters because I am way prettier than you."

"What? That flamingo neck womanizer has some nerve! I hope his tongue falls out whenever he goes to kiss you tonight."

"Judean! Why would you say that if it's true?" Marjorie picks up the cherry lip gloss off of the dresser and applies to her lips.

"Excuse me? Are you kidding me right now? And you are defending this jerk? I am your sister and you allowed him to talk about me like that?"

Marjorie turns around and stares into my eyes. "Judean, you are my sister and I love you. But you will NEVER be anything like me. I am what the boys like. I am beautiful, smart, nice figure, outgoing. You (as she looks at me up and down) ... well, you need to work on fixing yourself up some. You look so plain and unattractive. You look like you have no life in you. So yeah, Floyd was right in saying you are unattractive. You can't be mad at someone for speaking the truth, right?" Marjorie turned back around to pick up her purse off of the bed. "Don't wait up. Wish me luck!"

And just like that, Marjorie disappeared. She left me there with my confidence and my self-esteem dispersed all over the bedroom floor like garbage.

***

"That was a defining moment for me. Not only did I not have support from my mother, I had a sister that felt I was unworthy, also. I mean, I am flesh and blood. Seems like that should account for something, right? If someone you love is lacking in areas that are fixable, could you at least say something or try to help? Well, I suppose not. Marjorie was all about self. If it didn't have to do with her, it wasn't important."

"Dang Ma. Seems like you were surrounded by non-loving people. Just listening to you, how were you able to - I guess survive is a good word?" EJ asked.

"Son, I had a praying Grandmother."

CHAPTER SIX

"I never met my Great-Grandmother, right Ma?"

"No. She died way before you were born. That was the worst day of my life."

I got up and walked to the window facing the backyard. The neighbor's teenage son did a great job mowing the lawn. He forgot to edge the grass with the weed eater next to the fence. No big deal. I'm the only one that goes back there anyway. As I stood there gazing outside at the green grass, I felt a smile come across my face. I thought about the only woman who loved me, and it seemed like time stood still for just a moment. I can see Momma Jean sitting in the rocking chair on her front porch. It was hot that day. We didn't have anything to keep us cool other than that tall glass of lemonade and a church fan Momma Jean took from choir rehearsal. Just listening to my grandmother hum while rocking back and forth, I knew all was well in the world. The birds were chirping, and I could hear the frogs in the distance. I longed for those moments when it was just me and Momma Jean. Carolyn always left me with her when she had things to do with Marjorie. Which was fine by me. My grandmother was my peace. She always made me feel loved and wanted. I often wondered what would have become of me if there was no her.

***

"Momma Jean?"

"Yes, Shuga." Momma Jean didn't look up. She just held her head back with her eyes closed and kept rocking, hoping that the afternoon breeze would finally show up.

"Why doesn't Momma love me?"

Momma Jean stopped rocking and looked down at me as I sat on the top step of the porch. We met eye to eye. By this time, I had cried all of the tears I could cry. I had no tears left - no emotions. I just looked at her matter-of-factly waiting for an answer.

"Child, what in Gawd's name is you speakin' 'bout?"

"I heard you and Momma that night when she said she didn't want me." I felt my eyes burning, trying to well up with tears, but I kept them in. Momma Jean frowned and started rocking again.

"Baby, yo Momma loves ya. She juss don't show it 'cause she is mean as a snake." Momma Jean's frown just made a vein pop out on her forehead.

"No, she doesn't Momma Jean. I might be young, but I understood everything she said and it was perfectly clear what she meant. I would have rather not even been born than to know I am here and she doesn't love me."

Momma Jean, with her eyes closed, was silent for a few moments. I think she was praying because she mouthed the words 'Jesus'.

"Listen to me good child …" I see the sweat dripping from Momma Jean's face, down to her neck, down to the crease of her bosom. Clearly, I could see the agitation just by looking at the expression on her face. The mere fact that she had to talk with me about my mother was painful enough, however, she looked at me with such gentleness as she began to speak.

"You's been born here for a reason. Gawd don't make mistakes. Don't pay no mind to what yo Momma said. She's always been a mean sumthin." Momma Jean sucked her teeth. "Must have get it from her Pappy side of tha family."

"Momma Jean, I hate my life. I hate being called ugly. I hate being unloved by my own family… except you, I mean. I cry at night because I don't have a real purpose for being here. Sometimes, I wish I was dead because it hurts so bad. Besides… Momma won't care or miss me anyways." As I look down at the ground, I could feel how disappointed Momma Jean was when I said that.

Wide-eyed, my grandmother motioned me to come and sit between her legs. As I kneeled down in front of her, she laid my head across her chest and cried out to the Lord. I laid there and I cried on her already wet bosom. She prayed over me and began to sing one of the songs she always led at church. Momma Jean's voice bellowed as if she wanted to make sure God heard her.

As Momma Jean hugged me tight and wiped the tears from my eyes, she said to me, "Judean, baby, Gawd has a great purpose for ya. Ya don't know it yet, but He does. I loves ya with all my soul, Judean. Don't ya ev'va forget that your Momma Jean loves ya, hehn? But know that God loves ya mo' and mo' than anyone can. Don't ya listen to that devil talk about you wantin' dead. Go to Gawd when ya feelin' down. Gawd'll help ya through the bad times, baby. Ya henh me?"

"Yes, Momma Jean, I hear you." I hugged her a little tighter. "I love you so much. And thank you for loving me." She rocked me back and forth for what seemed like hours. A tranquil comfort like no other.

***

I was so deep in my thoughts, I thought I could actually smell her. My breathing was slow and steady and I felt like I was floating. By this time, EJ came over to me and hugged me. If he didn't, I think I would have passed out.

"You okay, Ma?" as he made sure to not to let me fall.

"Yes, son. Help me to the couch please." I dropped down on the couch like I was lifeless. I felt so lightheaded and distant. It still catches me off-guard sometimes to know that Momma Jean is gone. I can't shake her death. After all of these years, I am still afraid to let her go.

EJ was silent with a look of bewilderment on his face. I guess it was a shock to him knowing that his mother wanted to die. It's such an awful thing for anyone to hear without being judgmental. I hope he doesn't think any less of me. It's too late to take back my words now.

"Ma, if you sure you are okay, I am going to go to the bathroom. Do you need anything before I return?"

"No thank you. I'll be fine until you get back."

"Okay, be back in a few minutes."

As EJ walked out of the room, I began to pray. *"Lord, this was not my intent today… to go down memory lane. {sigh} Such bad memories I wanted to keep locked away. But I know I must complete this journey with EJ. I might as well finish what I started. No need in telling half-truths about my life. At this point, it is all or nothing. Lord, please be with me. I don't have the strength to do this by myself. You said in Your word, You would never leave me nor forsake me. Please, don't leave me now. In Jesus name, I pray…"*

Just then EJ walked around the corner.

"Amen."

"Did I interrupt your prayers, Ma?"

"No son. I just finished talking with the Lord." I smiled.

CHAPTER SEVEN

After gaining my composure, I started thinking about Annette. Oh, Annette… I thought about all of the things that make me really disturbed about you. But hey, she was there when no one else was. I can't quite put my finger on whether keeping her as a friend was good or not. "Humph."

I could feel the tightness of my face when EJ said, "Ma, what… or who… are you thinking about? Man, if looks could kill."

EJ wasn't really sure whether to smile or not. He had grabbed some cookies from the kitchen counter on his way back from the bathroom and devoured one before sitting down. "Want a cookie?" as he unfolded the napkin that had five cookies neatly stacked.

"Sure. Thank you." I reached for one cookie just to get the taste of coffee out of my mouth. That little bit of savory sweetness was all I needed.

"Son, I have a question for you? Do you have any close friends in college?"

"Nahhh… not *close* close. I have some associates that I hang out with, but no one I can call a close friend. Why do you ask?" He bit into his next cookie as reached down to pick up a crumb off of the floor.

"When I was in high school, I became friends with Annette. She wasn't like anyone I have ever encountered. She was a sheltered girl - her daddy being a preacher and all - and was really quiet in school. However, when we went to college and became roommates, that quiet sheltered girl became an entirely different person. They say that daughters of pastors are wild. I didn't believe it until I actually saw it for myself. My reserved friend became a …. what's the word you kids use today for fast girls?"

"A thot?" without hesitation nor looking away from his cookie.

"Yeah… that. Well, that is what she became, and I saw a whole different side to her. This one particular afternoon, she challenged every negative thought I had about her. And somehow, those thoughts came to fruition. We were both sitting in our dorm room studying … or attempting to study … and the conversation we had floored me."

Annette jumped out of her bed to answer the telephone alongside the wall in our room.

"Hello? Oh heeeeeeeey…. what's up?" She looked at me wide-eyed like a deer in headlights. "Fine by me. Which day and what time?" Annette turned her back towards me and finished her call. "Okay, I will see you then. Bye."

She hung up the phone and bounced back on top of her bed. She was about to put her headphones on when I asked her, "Who was that?"

"Oh, this guy I know who wanted to take me out. I said sure... why not. My exam isn't until Tuesday, so I can spare some time over the weekend." She was about to place the headphones on again when I asked, "Is it someone that I know?"

Annette could tell that I was not going to let this go so she sat up on the bed and looked at me.

"What? Why are you looking at me like that?" I asked.

"Deany, I have to tell you something."

Her expression was like *'let me tell her so she will stop questioning me'* look.

"Okay." I place my highlighter on the page where I left off and sat up over the edge of the bed. "What do you want to tell me."

"I want to tell you that I was asked out by Frank."

"Hold up. My Frank? The one I used to date, Frank?" Shocked was an understatement.

"Well... technically, he is not yours anymore. You guys have been broken up for what ... two months?"

"Seven weeks to be exact. What is up with that, Annette? Boys are dumb and don't care about anything but one thing. But you, whom I thought was my best friend, you are willing to date someone I used to date?"

"Look Deany. Again... you two are not dating anymore. And besides, you said you didn't like him that much because you two are not compatible. I figured since you have no interest in him like that anymore, why not go out with him? Is there a problem with that?"

***

I caught EJ's eyes anxiously awaiting my next statement. "My best friend just asked me if it was okay ... with me ... to start dating someone I held hands with, I shared my first kissed with, I spent nights ... (realizing I was talking to EJ, I caught myself before I said anything out of character) talking about the future with. I just couldn't believe she had the audacity to even think of such a thing. I mean, isn't there some woman code or best friend code that you should NOT date someone your girlfriend dated?"

EJ shook his head and agreed with me. "If they are a 'true' friend, there are some standards that you should abide by."

***

Getting back to Annette's question, *is there a problem with that?* My mind was still in process mode when I finally did open my mouth. "You know what Annette, you are absolutely right. I am no longer seeing Frank. And he has full rights to see whomever he wishes to see. If you are okay with dating someone I used to date, then go for it. They say one person's trash is another person's treasure." The level of sarcasm in my last statement could have cut a 2x4 in half with little effort.

"Alright. I knew you would understand." Then she came over and hugged me. And I felt disgusted, angry and betrayed.

***

"Wow, Ma… that right there is the ultimate disrespect. That was not cool at all. How were you able to cope with them dating?"

"I wasn't." I looked down at the floor. "I tried to avoid being around them as much as possible. I mean, they would actually kiss right in front of me and they didn't see anything wrong with that. That was the day when having a best friend became obsolete. Sure, I can still talk to her, but I will never, ever trust her again. Ever."

"Never in a million years would I have thought Auntie Annette would stoop that low. That's actually trifling."

"Yeah, well, you live and you learn, son. You have to learn to pick your battles. Some battles and some people are not worth it. That is why I gave her my blessing. If she would stoop that low towards me, her best friend, then she was not a friend to begin with. And therefore, they both deserved each other."

EJ, noticing my evil smile, started smiling himself and asked, "What are you smiling about?"

"I'm smiling because the two lovebird's relationship didn't last long anyway. It seems one of the two gave the other a 'gift' that only penicillin could cure."

Laughing hysterically, EJ yelled, "Yoooooo, what?"

The laughs between the both of us echoed within the entire room.

"Yeah… karma has no conscious about who it hurts." I think I smiled a little too hard at her misfortune, but God don't like ugly.

CHAPTER EIGHT

EJ and I laughed until we had tears. Different kinds of tears though. Laughing until you cry is good for the soul. Maybe I shouldn't have discussed Annette's 'party favor' with my son, but the story had to have somewhat of a happy ending, right? On a serious note though, I have to finish what I began. The four causes of my pain. Pain that I didn't know how to deal with except to just deal with it.

"I saved your father for last. As you can tell from the previous conversation that it wasn't only your father destroying my inner spirit. There were others. Seemed as if everyone except Momma Jean betrayed my love, confidence, and trust. The two most important people in my life... my mother and husband ... turned out to be the two people that hurt me the most. Elijah would be the one who destroyed what little self-respect I had in myself. He was my husband. We were supposed to be joined as 'one' after making a vow before God to love, honor and respect each other. I did my part. I gave my life to a man that I thought loved me. Looking back, he really didn't love me at all."

"Ma, I'm sure Dad loved you," EJ said in a convincing way to make it believable.

"No son, I am older now. I see things differently than when I was younger. Your father only married me out of convenience. I was single, no kids, I had my own place, a good job, and a car. He labeled me as 'Five Stars'. Back then, it sounded like a cute compliment. That's what opportunists do - they prey on the weak-minded. Now I know it was just a ploy to gain my interest." I frowned and snickered at the same time. "I guess it worked, huh?"

My smile disappeared, and the look of discontentment filled my eyes. "I remember the time God finally revealed to me that Elijah was cheating on me."

"Wait... what? Cheated? Are you being serious with me right now?" EJ grabbed his head and shook it in disbelief.

"Yes. I had always suspected something, but on this day, it was confirmed. Sometimes, God will smack you in the face just to catch your attention."

***

"Where are you going? It's Mother's Day."

"You are not my mother." Elijah's words pierced me like a switchblade. He might as well had cut me with one.

"I know I'm not your mother, Elijah, but can't you help your son celebrate me? He's only five years old."

"No. I have someplace else to go." Elijah got up out of the chair and walked towards the closet. He pulled a small pink gift bag out of his jacket pocket that was hidden from me.

"Is that for me?" as I looked wide-eyed with excitement and surprised at the beautiful pink bag he had in his hand.

"No."

"No?" I asked as the look of disappointment covered my face. "Then who is it for?"

"If you must know," as Elijah picked up the keys by the front door and turned halfway to look at me, "… it's for a friend."

"A friend? What friend are you —"

The door slams. The loudness of the door sent a jolt through my body like I was hit by a bullet from an automatic rifle. *'A friend'* echoed I my head as I tried to wrap my mind around the fact that he slammed the door in my face while I was mid-sentence. What kind of friend could make my husband leave me, the mother of his only son, alone on Mother's Day?

"Is he for real? Did this man just leave me to see another woman?" I muttered under my breath. I reached for the couch to brace my weakened knees from collapsing from under me. I could literally hear my heartbeat in my ears as the rage began to come over me. My neck began to pulsate with every beat. Satan himself must have entered my body because I know for a fact I saw fire.

"EJ!" I shouted.

The steps of small feet came running towards me. "Yes, Mommy?" His beautiful eyes looked concerned about my call.

"Can you please go to the refrigerator and get Mommy a bottle of water?"

"Ok, Mommy. I'll be right back!" My baby runs to the kitchen, happy to help me on my special day. Running back to me with a bottle of water in his tiny hands, Little EJ smiles and says, "Happy Mother's Day, Momma! Look at what I brought you."

I grabbed his chin, kissed him on the cheek and said, "Thank you, my sweet baby." I managed to smile to make him see my big gratitude towards this small favor.

Little EJ asks, "Where's Daddy?"

I tried my best to keep a frown from forming on my face. I said, "He went out. He'll be back later."

"Okay. Bye Momma!" Little EJ smiles back and runs back into his room to play.

Sitting on the couch, the tears began to form and swell in my eyes. That overwhelming feeling of rage was overshadowed by deep disappointment. *"Lord, what have I done to deserve this? Why would Elijah leave me and go to another woman? And on Mother's Day?"* I buried my hands in my face so my little boy would not hear my sobs in the other room. *"Oh God... why doesn't Elijah love me anymore?"*

Sobbing uncontrollably at this point, I realized I couldn't catch my breath. Inhale deeply.... exhale slowly. I repeated this until I could no longer hear my heartbeat. Swallowing what little pride and self-respect I had, I wiped my tears and began to pray to God. If I ever needed God, it was now. I knew it would take nobody but God to prevent me from taking what little I actually had to call my own, along with my little boy, and just walk away. To leave and don't look back. But I knew that EJ needed his father. It would have been selfish of me to take him away because I was the one being disrespected by Elijah. I asked the Lord to help me to deal with it because I couldn't do it by myself.

When I regained my composure, I managed to grab a tissue from the coffee table. I dried my eyes and fixed my makeup. The most important part of my life was in the other room. So innocent and oblivious to my heartache. And I was glad. I was adamant that EJ was not going to be susceptible to the kind of behavior that I receive from his Dad. He needed to see his Mother happy. As much as Elijah tried to break me, I couldn't let him destroy what little sense of self I had. He was not worthy of that. In fact, he was never worthy of it. But when I made that promise to God on my wedding day, for better or worse, I meant it. Even if I had to suffer being disrespected, I know God was going to take care of me. Momma Jean said so.

As I went to the kitchen to throw away the empty water bottle and tissue, I heard EJ laughing and giggling with his action figures. He told his little toys that today was Mother's Day and that he loved his Momma sooooo much. My heart smiled, and I sighed a big breath of relief. If I didn't know anything else in this world, I knew my only child loved me. I walked into EJ's room to find him on the floor surrounded by wrestling and football figurines. I got down on all fours and began to play with my only love.

The brightness of his eyes could light up an entire room, especially the darkness of my soul.

***

When I came back to reality, I saw EJ standing by the fireplace. He was staring at the family picture on the mantle with tears were streaming down his face. I walked over and hugged him.

CHAPTER NINE

"Momma, I'm so sorry," EJ sobbed. "I had no idea this is what you went through with Dad. I feel so bad and helpless right now because I can't do anything now to change what happened." EJ banged the edge of the chair arm so hard, I thought he had broken his wrist. I could see the fury in his eyes.

"Son, listen, that was not your cross to bear. My job was to take care of you, not the other way around." I took my hand and lifted EJ's chin so that his eyes could see mine. "I did not tell you these things to get you upset. You asked me about my past. I gave you an uneasy description of some of my pain. To be quite frank, if I had told you everything, our talk would last all night into tomorrow."

"That still does not help the anger I feel inside because I couldn't help you, Ma. I know I was a child and all, but I could have been more supportive as I got older. I just didn't know. And I'm sorry."

"Now stop! You have absolutely nothing to apologize for. Like you said, you were a child. And I tried to do everything in my power to make sure you were a happy child. Even if it meant that I had to suffer. And I would do it all over again if I had to."

"Why didn't you tell anyone? Couldn't anyone help you? I mean, even with Momma Jean... couldn't she find help for you in some way when you told her you didn't want to live?"

"Back then, EJ, that was something we didn't talk about. Folks didn't talk about depression or feeling sad. And definitely not suicide."

As I looked away from his eyes, I felt somewhat embarrassed for even saying that to my son.

"People would say it was the devil talking in your head. I just had to 'pray it out of me' or 'get over it'. I was too hurt to pray, so I just got over it. Am I proud of that? No. However, I had no other choice. And besides, I didn't want to talk with anyone because I didn't want to be judged or I didn't want people to think I was crazy. All I wanted was to be loved. I can honestly say, the only love I felt was from Momma Jean and you. You two were and are my reasons for living. Even though Momma Jean has been gone for years, sometimes I can sense her presence during my weakest moments."

"Ma," EJ grabbed my hands and firmly squeezed them. "I need you to promise me something."

"What is it?"

"I want you to promise me that you will seek counseling to talk about your past."

"Son..."

"No - no, now I am serious with you. You have experienced some traumatic events in your life that you have not resolved. Ma, your emotional feelings have been covered up and festered over the years and your mental state can't take any more bad experiences. Please understand what I am saying. Back when you were growing up, they didn't have counseling or therapy for depression. They do now. There are plenty of support groups to take advantage of for people who suffered in silence."

"You're right. I would have been called weak and even worse, I would have been straight institutionalized if I talked about needing help. The word depression was taboo. No one talked about it."

"And that is why it is important right now. You have options, Ma. Help is available to you in so many forms. Please, for me. Go see a professional."

Looking at my son, I felt the presence of Momma Jean. She always wanted the best for me. She always prayed for me. And here it is - my son - looking out for my well-being. I know he loves me. More importantly, he also cares.

"Okay son. I promise."

After our talk, EJ was mentally exhausted himself so he decided to stay the night. I was thankful because I didn't want to be alone. I sent EJ to bed since he had to get on the road early in the morning. I finished cleaning up the kitchen. It wasn't much to do anyway. Neither one of us felt hungry enough to eat after our talk. We both decided to just retire for the evening.

I walked into my bedroom, took off my clothes and sat at the vanity ... naked. I proceeded to comb my hair and wipe the makeup from my face. I looked at myself for a long time. I just stared. I normally don't look at myself to see what other people see. I've always felt so unattractive. Unworthy. But at this particular moment, I actually wanted to see what I looked like. My eyes were light brown. I always thought they were darker. Maybe they appeared darker because all I ever saw was darkness. My skin was the perfect shade of creamy chocolate. *'If I stood next to a wood-burning fire, I might melt'* I smirked to myself. I ran my fingers over my face, neck shoulders, arms…. and my skin felt like a newborn baby's bottom - full and smooth to the touch. My breast and thighs were 'fluffier' than the average woman. I am definitely not model material, but I am proportionally curved. I smiled at what I saw. Wow. I am a beautiful woman.

If you are so beautiful, why didn't Elijah want you?

"Satan," I called his name sternly, "You will not destroy this moment for me. Go back to hell from whence you came."

And with that, I got up and headed to the shower. On my way, I stopped at the wall mirror to view myself. I smiled, then proceed to the shower stall. I turned the water on and made sure it was lukewarm, just cool enough to satisfy the mini hot flash that was about to creep up on me. With my eyes closed, I imagined all of my burdens washing off of me and going down the drain. I cried tears of relief as the weight was lifted. Because my body experienced overwhelming weakness, I slid down the shower wall into a seated position. I've been holding on to burdens for so long, being weightless was overpowering. *"God, I thank you.*

I never thought I could feel so free. And it took my only child to release me from some of my sorrows. Thank you, Lord, for my son. Thank you, Lord, for loving me enough to release the heaviness in my heart and in my spirit. And thank you, Lord, for loving me enough to bless me with another day."

That night was the first restful sleep I have had in years.

CHAPTER TEN

I walked into the church, nervous like I have never been there before. When I walked in, the administration building smelled 'holy' like frankincense and myrrh. The sound of gospel music echoed throughout the halls. I reached Pastor Benson's office fifteen minutes ahead of our scheduled appointment time.

"Good morning, Sista Judean! How are you this morning?" Sista Pauline got up from her desk at the receptionist area to greet me with a hug.

"Good morning, Sista Pauline. I am doing well. How about yourself?" I asked as I hugged her back.

"I am blessed and highly favored all thanks to our Almighty God." She smiled like she didn't have any worries. "It is so good to see you. You are radiant today. God broke the mold when he made your beautiful face."

Not sure whether to take her compliment seriously or whether I just can't accept a compliment. "Thank you." I smiled. "I appreciate your kinds words."

"I will let Pastor Benson know you are here."

"Thank you." I sat on one of the chairs nervously awaiting to talk to Pastor. He had been wanting to talk with me since the passing of Elijah. I just couldn't bring myself to do it. But here I am. I wasn't waiting long before this tall man, wearing what looked like a navy-blue Armani suit, walked from around the corner.

"Sista Judean! What a blessing it is to see you." With outstretched arms, this handsome older gentleman came before me. I felt myself smiling just a little too much. And good Lord, I didn't realize Pastor Benson was this handsome up close.

As I stood up, I could feel my cheeks burning from the smile etched across my face. "Good morning, Pastor Benson. It's good to see you as well."

As I hugged Pastor, I could smell his cologne. OH, MY GOD! Lord, you know I should NOT be thinking about such things like this. This is my Pastor for God's sake. But whew, he feels so good. Jesus keep me near the cross. Get yourself together, Judean. This is a man of the cloth. Have mercy on my soul! Judean, girl stop! Just stop and let go of him. When I got married, I never looked at other men in *that* way. I was a committed woman. Have mercy, I never realized how seasoned and fine Pastor was. His beard was fully gray and neatly groomed. Underneath his glasses were hazel brown eyes... those mesmerizing eyes.

"You are looking radiant today, my dear." Pastor said as he had unknowingly broken my trance.

"I told her the exact same thing, Pastor!" exclaimed Sista Pauline as she smiled at me. Her quick side glance said *'Girl, you betta get that man before someone else does'*. She gave me a wink and walked away to give us some privacy.

"Thank you, Pastor."

"Come on this way to my office." As Pastor led me down the hallway, Sista Pauline, once again, gave me a side grin. I have to admit, I was tickled.

Pastor took off his suit coat and placed it on a hanger as soon as we walked into his office. I sat down on the couch and Pastor was about to sit in the adjacent chair next to me when he asked, "Would you like something to drink?"

"Oh, no thank you. Ummm… well… yes, please. A bottle of water would be great. Thank you." I better get that water in case Pastor get me choked up as I talk. Internally, I'm still smiling at how Pastor greeted me. This man is fine. Pastor brought a bottle of water and a napkin and placed it on the end table between us. As he sat down in his chair, I secretly wished he would sit next to me.

"Judean, how is Elijah Jr. doing? Is he still attending that school in Georgia?"

"Yes, sir. EJ is doing great and ready to finish out his last two semesters of college. He came up to visit me on Sunday after church. Which is why I came to see you today."

"It's great to hear that young man is doing so well. I am very proud of him and the man he is becoming. Are you saying EJ is the reason why you came today? How so?"

"Well Pastor, EJ and I had a very serious conversation and he seems to think I am depressed."

"And what do you think?" His question came abruptly.

"Pastor, when I talked to EJ about my past, I realized that I had been holding a lot of old hurt, anger, and resentment for the last forty-five plus years. And that is a long time to keep things in. But you know as well as I do, we couldn't talk about being sad and depressed back when we were growing up."

"That's true. However, you didn't answer my question. Do you think you are depressed?" There goes that stern look he gave me during the Sunday sermon. As he peered over his glasses, that's the Pastor I recognized.

"Honestly, I don't know. I've felt this way for as long as can remember. I am used to it, so it has become a norm for me."

"Let me talk to you as a man for a moment, not as a Pastor. When my wife died, I died too. This woman was my entire world, my soul mate, if you will. I can honestly say that I questioned God briefly because my grief took over my flesh. I couldn't eat, I couldn't sleep, and I spiraled into a deep depression that I really didn't think I would get out of. The woman that I loved was gone forever and never to come back on this earthly side. That was something I could not grasp. I took a leave of absence from pastoring because I needed to heal. And I needed professional help in dealing with my grief. I thank God for wisdom in knowing what was wrong with me to ask for help. Losing a spouse is not easy."

"I agree, Pastor. But my anguish goes way beyond the death of Elijah."

Pastor sat back and stared at me intently. "What do you mean, Sista?"

As I proceeded to tell Pastor the same story I told EJ, talking about my life seem to make me feel a little lighter than before. That small pinprick into my soul excreted more bottled up pressure from my past. This time, though, I was able to talk without crying. It felt good. A relief. Pastor listened the entire time without interruption. His eyes never wavered. His body never moved. I was so much more at peace talking to him. After I was finished explaining, I looked into his eyes. I was not sure of what his thoughts were going to be towards me. He just stared for what seemed like hours even though it was just mere seconds.

Pastor moved his chair in front of where I was sitting and opened up his hands. "Take my hands."

As I gave Pastor my hands, they shook a little. But he grabbed them for dear life. His grasp was strong, yet his hands were soft. Pastor closed his eyes and bowed his head.

"Most gracious heavenly Father, I come before you with your child Judean, as humbly as I know how. Oh God, I give thanks for deliverance. I give thanks for healing. I thank you in advance, God, for what you are about to do in Sista Judean's life. Her life was filled with lack of love, many disappointments, ill-treatment, and misunderstandings. But God, only You know why those things happened. They all happened for a reason. Manifest those reasons so that Judean can use them for Your glory. Lord, continue to bless this woman so that she can heal, be happy and move on with her life. For she has so much more living to do.

God, You are the author of her life. Help her to realize that she is the head and not the tail and You will never leave her nor forsake her. Thank you, Jesus. These and all other blessings I ask for her sake, O God. In your Son Jesus' name, I do pray. Amen."

"Amen," I said. As I looked up, Pastor Benson was smiling at me.

"God has a blessing in store for you, Judean. Sometimes we have to go through the bad just to have a greater appreciation for the good. And it is coming your way. Continue to trust God like Momma Jean told you to do. Trust and believe. You will still have the devil get in your way from time to time. And that is okay because that's his job. You just remember to remain faithful and diligent. Always remind yourself that you are beautiful, you deserve better and you do matter."

"Thank you, Pastor. These last few days since EJ came to visit have been so peaceful. I can literally feel the weight lifted off. I often think that I wasted so much time not talking about this sooner."

"Judean, leave the past right where it is - behind you. You can't change it. Focus on the right now and move forward. Besides, back then wasn't your time to talk about it. Your time is now. And with that being said, I do have another appointment I have to attend in forty-five minutes across town. I apologize, I must end our conversation now."

"Oh, my Lord, Pastor, I didn't realize I talked for over an hour. I apologize for taking up so much of your time."

"Sista Judean, it was my pleasure. And God allowed this to happen for a reason. Don't apologize for that."

We both got up from our chairs. As Pastor put his chair back into its space, I grabbed the bottle of water and drank half of it. It was as refreshing as Pastor's prayer.

"Sista, one other thing." Pastor reach for his suit jacket on the hanger and put it on. "I would like for you to attend a depression group that I sponsor at the Women's Mission for the Homeless on Saturday nights. I speak to men and women who are in need of counseling, among other things, and I think you would really benefit from listening to them. Several people that I speak with have similar stories and it would be a great opportunity for you to listen and possibly become a mentor. So, I extend my invitation out to you."

"Thank you. I would love to." I said as I placed my purse on my shoulder.

"Great. I will have Sista Pauline to contact you with the information and I look forward to seeing you on Saturday." Pastor reached over and gave me a hug. "God bless you, Judean. You hold on to your faith. Your blessing is on the way."

As I looked up to him, our eyes met. Bashfully I said, "Thank you so much, Pastor. I appreciate your time. And I will see you on Saturday."

I walked down the hall feeling a lot lighter than when I came in. Sista Pauline was not at the front desk. Good. I didn't want her seeing the girlish grin on my face as I walked out of the door.

That night after my meeting with Pastor Benson, Annette sends me a text to hang out on Thursday night. Why not? It's not like I have some sort of schedule to go by. The last few days, I have been feeling exhilarated. This feeling of floating on clouds is so remarkable. I can close my eyes and the sense of peace is so overwhelming. It almost scares me because I am always expecting the worst. Why haven't I let all of this go a long time ago? I could have been happier sooner. I can only assume I wasn't ready to receive it. Or God wasn't ready for me to receive it. I don't know. Either way, I am at this happy time now. And that is all that matters.

CHAPTER ELEVEN

Annette will be here soon. I walked into the closet and rummaged through my clothes. *I need a new wardrobe,* I thought to myself. Everything looks so old and beat up, just like my inner thoughts used to be. I need something to match my awakened spirit. Sigh. I grabbed a pair of jeans and multi-colored blouse. I haven't worn heels in a minute, so I decided on wedged heels. At least I can balance myself while walking as I get back into presenting myself more like a woman.

I looked at myself in the mirror as I applied pressed powder to my face, eyeshadow, mascara, and lip gloss as a finishing touch. I was never one to use a lot of makeup. What was the purpose? I was nothing to admire. Or so I thought. But now, when I look in the mirror, I still get taken aback by what I see. I am happy about what I see in myself. My face appears 'lighter' as if my inner self is glowing. It is glowing. I stood up and walked over to the wall mirror. *"Judean, you are beautiful. You are classy. You are sexy. You are what God made you to be. Nothing more, nothing less. And… you are also crazy for talking to yourself in the mirror."* I shook my head and I smiled at myself. My smile. Something else to add to my list of likes about myself.

Knock-knock-knock

That must be Annette. Late as usual. I hurried to the front door. When I opened the door, Annette stood there flabbergasted.

"Are you going to just stand there with your mouth open or are you going to come in?"

"Whoa Deany? What did you do? Did you have a makeover session and didn't call your girl?"

"Well, it's nice to see you, too."

"Deany, seriously. You look great!" Annette leaned over and gave me a hug and walked inside.

Annette walked over to the living room and started rambling about her new love interest.

"Girl, let me tell you about this guy I met. He's fit and fine. But only one small problem. We literally see each other eye to eye."

"Oh, you mean he is five feet nine like you?"

"Nah…. He's five feet eight and a half. But I think I can overlook that. Ummm…. no pun intended."

I laughed so hard I caught a cramp. I sat on the couch so I could finish listening to this story and to switch out purses while Annette talked about her guy.

"You are laughing, but I am dead serious. He's young, too. But we won't get into just how Cougar-ish I am." Annette gave me the side-eye, expecting me to say something. All I did was look down and began to count my cash. "Hey, no judgment here." I said as I still laughed under my breath.

"Deany, you know I'm not as young as I used to be. So that's why I am gonna turn up until I die!" I nearly fell out of my chair as I see Annette trying to drop it like it's hot…but somehow, she needed help getting up.

"You keep dropping it like that and you are gonna dislocate that right hip." Both of us couldn't control our laughter as Annette kept shifting positions to get that lifeless feeling out of her knees.

"Don't hate, Deany!" Now she is trying to twerk without using her lower legs.

"You are such a trollop!"

"And Imma be a trollop until my last breath."

"Okay…… okay," holding both hands up and closing my eyes. "Please stop. I don't need that visual." As we looked at each other for several seconds, we both collapsed on each other as we laughed hysterically. My God… I haven't laughed like that in years. Decades. That laugh came from so far within, it actually felt good.

"Welp, I've worked up a sweat so I'm going to run to the bathroom. Don't miss me too much while I'm gone." Annette walked to the bathroom while holding her back.

"Hahaha…. there is some Ibuprofen in the medicine cabinet."

"Very funny."

My relationship with Annette is manageable. Even though she deceived me in college, I still consider her as a friend. At least Annette was honest about what she did with my old boyfriend. Most women these days would lie in your face about their intentions.

***

The movie was great. No crying… strictly laughter. That's the best thing about comedy. Even when it's not funny, it's funny. I can't remember the last time I actually laughed, and I 'felt' it. I had almost forgotten what stomach cramps from laughing too hard felt like. I've been feeling so free over the last few days, it's too immense to describe. As Annette and I walked in the city - and talked and cackled and danced and acted like teenagers - my mind began to process what 'life' feels like. I was happy. I feel like a newborn who has taken its first breath.

We stopped at a local hole in the wall for some southern food. As we sat there, Annette drinking her usual libations and I'm drinking a ginger ale, we began to reminisce about our younger days. I felt a twitch in the pit of my stomach. My past is a sore subject, but I tried to be as supportive as possible. Annette noticed my facial expression change.

"Why so glum, chum?"

"It's nothing. I just don't like talking about my past. No good memories for me back there." My eyes felt a little moist but not enough to cry. I was not going to ruin my great evening over something I can't change at this point.

"Your past? What are you talking about? Your Mom?"

"It's a mixture of things Annette that I really don't want to talk about. Not tonight. However, I feel like I am on my way to healing from my past. I thank God for EJ and Pastor Benson. Those two really have helped me to acknowledge my hurt and I am ready to get my life back on track."

"Helped you?" Annette said that like she was offended that she didn't know what was going on about me. As one of my past stressors, why would I talk to her after what she did to me? "Deany, I didn't even know you were hurt other than your relationship with your mother. There's more?"

"Yes, but again, I don't want to get into that" I smiled. "Just know I'll be okay. Pastor Benson invited me to a depression group on …"

"Depression? Deany… what? Depression? You've never been depressed."

But this time, I was getting a little agitated that she would 'think' she knew how I have been feeling. "Annette, I have been depressed for a number of years now. I never told anyone because I was in denial myself. So yes, I have been depressed. I guess that means you never really paid attention to me either, huh?"

Annette's expression told it all - that ole 'deer in the headlights' look. Not only was she shocked by my question, she was shocked because she really didn't have a good response to my question. "Deany, I-I-I honestly…. Ummm, I suppose …. I guess I didn't. I'm sorry. I-I didn't know."

"Annette, it's okay. Even if you did know, there wasn't anything you could do about it anyway. Besides, it wasn't your responsibility to care for my mental health. It was mine."

By this time, the tears were streaming down Annette's cheeks like she just lost someone close. I have never seen her cry. So, I can't quite figure out if the tears are truly genuine.

"I'm so sorry Judean. I was a horrible friend to you. I was always thinking of myself and all of this time, you were dealing with things I didn't know about. Because I was all about me. Oh, my God… please forgive me?" She got up out of her seat and slid next to me on my side of the booth. She hugged me so tight, I think it left an imprint of my necklace on my neck. "I love you, Deany."

Wow… I have never heard those words from her either.

"I love you, too, Annette." We both exchanged glances and smiles. I grabbed a tissue off of the table and blotted her eyes. I am so proud of myself. I didn't shed a tear. "Now, please get back to your seat before people think we are lovers."

Both of us giggled so loudly it echoed inside the restaurant. People were looking at us. I think a few laughed at us, not know what we were laughing about.

When Annette slid back into her seat, our food came. Just in time. I didn't want to feel that 'awkwardness' between us. As we ate, there was a little bit of silence. It hit her a little bit harder than I expected. Which was kind of weird because Annette never let things get under her skin. She broke the silence when she started talking about her nieces and nephews. What a pleasant distraction.

***

Annette drove me back home. I honestly didn't want to go home but we both had a long day. And I know that Annette was still somewhat emotional from the evening.

"Annette, I never did finish telling you about the depression group I was invited to on Saturday. It is at the Gospel Mission. This is going to be my first time there and to be quite honest, I don't want to go alone. If you don't have anything to do, would you please go with me?"

"Deany, of course I will. Text me the address and time and I will be there."

"Great. Thank you. And I will. Good night and drive safely."

"I had a great evening. Good night."

I walked to my door, unlocked it and stepped in. As I looked back, Annette waved and I caught a sliver of shiny light on her face. She was crying again.

I waved and closed the door behind me.

CHAPTER TWELVE

The air is a little crisp tonight. I'm glad I brought my sweater. Or maybe I have a little chill inside my soul. Being a newbie at this depression group meeting that Pastor Benson invited me to is out of my element. I've never ventured on that side of town, so I am sure I won't know anyone there. I'm glad Annette agreed to go with me.

I sat in the parking lot of the Gospel Mission to gather my thoughts. I also wanted to say a prayer. Lord, you know I have never been to any kind of group like this because … well … I just haven't. Keep me in perfect peace. And please keep me from having an anxiety attack in front of those strangers. More importantly, Lord, thank you for blessing me. I am finally on my way to healing. I've enjoyed the peace I have felt in the last few days. It has been a feeling like no other.

Just as I was ending my silent prayer, I see Pastor Benson walk to the door. He held the door open for a woman and then another couple approached just as he was about to step inside. Pastor Benson stepped back outside to hold the door for the guests. He shook the other man's hand and closed the door as he walked in. Such a gentleman.

Annette pulled into the parking space next to me. She smiled as she drove up. I gathered my purse and sweater and made my way out of the car.

"Hey Deany!" as she hugs me and touches my hair. I put my hair up into a perfectly tight puff. "I love the hair."

"Hey, Annette. Thank you."

"So, are you ready to do this?" Annette extends out her arm for me to interlock into hers.

"Let's do this," I said as I grabbed her arm. I've never felt as close to Annette as I do right now. My heart was bursting with happiness.

We walked inside and a small hallway led into the dining hall, we were greeted by a woman handing out pamphlets.

"Hello, ladies… welcome! Is this your first time here?" asked the woman very warmly.

"Yes. My name is Judean and this is my friend Annette."

"Very nice to meet you, ladies. We will be starting very shortly. Please feel free to walk around and introduce yourselves."

"Thank you," Annette and I said in unison.

Just as I was about to walk to the table with the light refreshments, Pastor Benson calls my name.

"Sista Judean!" Pastor Benson was walking over with his arms out for his usual church hug. This time, his hand was placed a little lower on my back than usual. Have mercy. Annette could not be more obvious as she glared at Pastor Benson. I read her lips. 'Oh my-y-y-y'.

"So glad you made it. Glory to God. And I see you brought someone with you. Good evening, young lady. I am Pastor Benson. And you are?"

Seeing that Annette couldn't form words, I answered for her. "Pastor, this is my girlfriend Annette. Annette, this is my Pastor from church, Pastor Benson."

"Sista Annette, it is a pleasure to meet you." Pastor extended out his hand to shake Annette's then gently leaned to give her a church hug, too. "You must come and fellowship with us sometime. You are certainly most welcome."

"Thank you, Pastor. I most certainly will." Annette smiled so hard you could see her silver fillings in the back of her mouth (rolling my eyes).

Clearing my throat, "So, where do we sit Pastor?" as I tried to take the focus away from Annette's wavering eyes and Chessy Cat grin.

Pastor said, "Please excuse us for a moment, Sista Annette, while I speak with Judean for just a moment."

"Sure Pastor. Deany, I'll go grab us a seat." Annette said… still smiling.

"Thanks, Annette." as I stretched my eyes at her as if to say, 'please stop gawking at this man like a sixteen-year-old'. Annette laughed and walked over to the seats in the main area and started talking with the couple I saw walk in earlier.

"Sista Judean, I am really glad to see you tonight."

"Thank you, Pastor. I think it will benefit me to be around people who suffer and share experiences like I do."

"I couldn't agree more. Since this is your first time, I don't expect you to say anything and please don't feel like you have to. This group is mainly for those who don't have anyone else they can talk to about their problems. Some don't have the insurance to cover the professional help they need. So, there are professionals here who volunteer their time to listen to others. And they help as much as they can outside of working hours. I am also glad you brought some support with you. You shouldn't deal with this alone. I am proud of you for taking that first step."

"Thank you, Pastor." I hope Pastor doesn't notice me blushing.

"And please, you may call me Phillip."

Interesting. I normally see the religious side of Pastor Benson. Today, I saw the man.

"Thank you, Phillip." Pastor Benson and I locked eyes for a few seconds and was then interrupted by a tapping on the microphone.

I see the woman we met at the door up front shuffling papers at the podium. "We will begin in about ten minutes everyone," she announced. I went and sat down next to Annette. She introduced me to the couple she was talking to. Just as we were exchanging greetings, the front door flung open. A woman wearing jeans and a tight-fitting t-shirt appeared inside. When she turned around, I was surprised to see the woman wearing the baseball cap with her ponytail out of the back to be Sista Patrice. No make-up, no breast popping out ... just plain old Patrice. Pastor Benson greeted Sista Patrice at the door since the door greeter was at the podium. I could tell by her demeanor that she was ashamed of how she looked in front of Pastor. I must say, she looked like she had a rough day. I've had that look ... plenty of times. Sista Patrice sat down on the other side of Annette, three seats over towards the window. I leaned over and said hello to Sista Patrice.

"Oh, h-h-hey." like she had never seen me before. "How are you?"

"I am doing well. How are you?"

"I'm fine. Thank you." With that, she leaned back in her seat and pretending to look for something in her purse.

"Deany," Annette whispered, "I've seen that chick before? You said her name is Patrice?"

"Yes, she goes to my church. She hasn't been there long, though. I really don't know much about her."

Annette and Patrice caught a quick glance at each other, gave a quick smile, then turn away.

"I've seen her somewhere before," Annette mumbled.

"Attention everyone. We will get started now. It is a Saturday night. Some of you may have plans for the rest of this evening. But if you are like me, you will be heading home to slip into some pajamas, lay on the couch and watch cable for the rest of tonight." said the door greeter.

Some small laughter rang out from everyone. Sista Patrice only managed to crack a glimmer of a smile.

"You got that right." A small framed lady that sat near the front shouted. "My partying days BEEN over."

Laughter. It was good to see people with a sense of humor in this type of setting.

"Good evening" said the door greeter as she stood at the podium. "For those who are here for the first time or for those who don't remember me from a few weeks ago, my name is Dr. Charlene Jackson-Jeffers and I am a Licensed Psychiatrist. And please, you can call me Dr. J.J. for short. I have been a practicing psychiatrist for twelve years. I have had my own practice for nine years here in town. The pamphlets I gave to you at the door have my office information located on the back and also a card attached in case you would like to make an appointment. I was invited here tonight to talk about a serious problem we have in the African-American community on how to deal with mental health. Mental health is a word that no one in our community wants to discuss. But I am here to tell you, it is real. It is prevalent. And it is harmful if not treated. Not only to the individual but to that individual's family and friends. So, it is not just a one-person problem. It is everyone's problem. Everyone just imagine this. Approximately 7.5 million African Americans have been diagnosed with a mental illness. 7.5 million! Just imagine the number of folks who have not been diagnosed. Either because of a lack of insurance that would cover the doctor visits or maybe even because of the stigma associated with the word 'mental'. One would think that depression, being bi-polar, and other mental health issues are a sign of weakness. And it could be portrayed as shameful. Think about it… do you ever remember a time when you really wanted to talk to someone and you choose a certain family member or friend to hear your concerns? Only to be told 'deal with it' or 'that's the devil messing with your mind' or 'you sound weak - you are stronger than that' or 'pray about it'? Let me see your hands if you have heard that or something similar."

Hands were raised and mumbles were heard. I have heard every one of those statements. Even Annette raised her hand in agreement.

"Okay. Seeing all of the hands raised just confirms what I am trying to relay to you. Our ancestors are stereotyped as being strong and being able to handle oppressive situations. They had no other choice. But you are not your ancestors. You have the ability to reach out and get the help you need. Let me ask you all a question. When you think of the word depression, what comes to mind?"

The man whom Pastor met at the door raised his hand. "Failure comes to my mind."

"Good answer." Dr. J.J. approved.

"Hopelessness." Pastor Benson answered.

"Thank you, Pastor. Anyone else?"

I raised my hand. All eyes were on me. "Sadness all of the time."

"Absolutely! All of these answers are correct. The thing about depression is that you just can't turn it off like a light switch. All of these feelings of failure, hopelessness, and sadness cannot be shaken off. And I may get a stern talking to after I say this," as Dr J.J. looks over at Pastor Benson, "but sometimes you can't pray it away either. And I stress the word sometimes."

The lady up front said, "That's true."

Pastor Benson smiled and nodded his approval of the statement.

"I will admit. Sometimes you could be under a spiritual warfare when it comes to spirits of depression. And prayer will be needed. That was not my point when I say you can't pray it away. My point is that depression sometimes will come from the physiological aspect of the 'earthly' body also. There are many different reasons why you can be depressed, such as chemical imbalances in the brain, certain medications that can alter your mood, genetics - especially if your immediate family has a history. Life events such as a death or a birth or even moving to a new city can trigger depression. Just dealing with life is a stressor."

"Deany, this is really good information," Annette leaned over and whispered. I nodded in agreement.

"I am not up here to take up too much time. I just wanted to say to you all that there is help. You don't have to deal with this alone. Do what you must to get the help that you need. Go to your physician, seek counseling and also consider medical therapy. And if you have any questions after this meeting, please feel free to come and see me before you leave. Thank you."

Hand claps echoed throughout the dining hall. As I clapped, I felt a sense of calmness because I was among people who are going through the same issues as I am. Dr. J.J. removed her papers as Pastor Benson walked up to the podium. Dr. J.J. walked to the back of the room to grab some punch from the punch bowl.

"Dr. J.J., thank you for being here this evening. And I appreciate each one of you for being here as well. Depression is a hard subject to talk about as the Doctor stated. But we must seek help to overcome this disease. Amen?"

"Amen," said everyone in the room.

"Before we begin, I would like to acknowledge our first-timers. If you would just please stand and if you would like to say something, you can. If not, it's quite alright."

I stood up and again, all eyes were on me. Nervous that I will stumble on my words, I took a deep breath, "Good evening everyone."

"Good evening," everyone replied.

"My name is Judean. And this is my friend Annette who came out to support me. This is my first time here and I thank you for having me."

Hand claps and welcomes gave me a warm, feel-good-all-over sensation.

"Thank you, Judean and welcome to you and Annette."

As I sat down, Annette took my hand and squeezed it. She smiled at me like I had just won an award.

CHAPTER THIRTEEN

"Moving right along," Pastor Benson stated, "we are now at the point of the night where you have an opportunity to share your thoughts with the group. We are not here to judge. We are here to listen and support our fellow members. Would anyone like to volunteer to speak first?"

"I would Pastor." The man who came in with the woman stood up and walked up to the podium. He was a tall man but looked a little frail, like he had not been eating or taking care of himself. He shook Pastor's hand once again. Then he leaned over to adjust the microphone.

"Good evening all."

"Good evening," everyone said in unison.

"My name is Eddie and I came out tonight with my wife Lorie. I am not new to this group; however, this will be my first time speaking. I got up enough nerve to stand up tonight because... well, it's time. It's time for me to accept what is and get the help I need. Not only for myself but for my lovely wife. Several years ago, I served in Desert Storm. I was young, adventurous and so full of life. In 1990, I was fresh out of high school and eager to serve the country I so desperately love. Before my deployment, I married the love of my life." The way that Eddie looked at his wife was with so much adoration. Something I wish I felt with my own husband. To be loved like that must be truly an indescribable feeling.

Eddie continued. "I only served 4 years. And that's because… um ……" Eddie looked down for several seconds so he could regain his composer.

"Um…. my time in the Middle East was not very good. And uh …. I saw a lot of things that …."

Now Eddie seemed like he was going to really fall apart if he finished his statement. But this time, his wife got up and stood beside her husband. She gently touched his arm as if to console him and let him know she would always be by his side. She didn't say a word. She didn't have to. Her touch and her presence said everything.

After clearing his throat, Eddie continued, "Excuse me. Sometimes talking about it gets hard."

"That's alright baby. Take your time," said the woman up front.

"Eddie?" By this time Dr. J.J. intervened. "Would you like to stop?"

"No… no, thank you. I have to learn to accept it for what it is and stop internalizing it. I got it. Thank you, Doctor."

Eddie looked up as he inhaled deeply. He stared at the side window so that he could not see the wide eyes of every person in the dining hall looking back at him.

"I saw a lot of things that no one should ever witness in their lifetime. I saw people getting killed, even women and children. I witnessed a convoy of five trucks ahead of me blow up before my very own eyes. The lives of three men were lost behind that attack. Men I had just had lunch with not an hour before. Needless to say, being a young man who had never grown up to such violence really took a toll on me after coming home. I couldn't close my eyes without seeing a small child being shot by a bullet. I cringe at every holiday that promotes fireworks. It would sound like rounds of bullets ringing out and I could not stop it. I couldn't eat or sleep." Eddie looked over at his wife. "My issues were very concerning to my wife. And rightfully so. Sometimes, she would find me in the middle of the night crouched down in the corner of my bedroom with my eyes closed and hand over my ears to drown out the sounds I thought I heard. I scared her. I was scared of myself. I was supposed to be the one protecting her, and I couldn't even…"

Eddie sniffed and his wife rubbed his arm once again and gave him another warm smile. "It was at that time that Lorie gave me the *'you are going to the see doctor or else'* look. I'm sure you all know that look I'm talking about."

Several chuckles were heard. "Well, I didn't want to go because I was afraid of what they would tell me. What they would think of me… I mean, here I am… a grown man who would tense up at the very sound of a doorbell. All and all, I am certainly glad she convinced me to go because I was diagnosed with PTSD, Post Traumatic Stress Disorder."

The woman up front mumbled, "Oh my Lord."

"I've had this problem for years but never sought the help I needed. I struggled over time and lost some very precious moments all because of fear. Sometimes I feared leaving my home. I dreaded the outside world. I have been going to therapy at the military hospital for a few months now. But you know, their sessions only last about an hour. And to be quite honest, I feel like I need more time to talk about my thoughts and feelings and to also listen to other folks who have similar situations stemming from traumatic events. I cannot lie, folks. This has been a long, tiresome and slow journey. But I trust God and am so very blessed to have a wife that loves and supports me. She has been my rock and my peace during this troublesome time in my life. Our lives. And for that, I want to publicly tell her THANK YOU!" Eddie turned to his wife, kissed her on the forehead and wrapped his arms around her.

As the hands were being clapped and the tissue box was being passed around, the couple stood there in their embrace like they were in their own little world. It was beautiful to see such a supportive wife. I can only imagine how hard it must have been for her as well. She was literally watching the man she loved fall apart. Honestly, I think I am tearing up more because I didn't have that support from my own husband. Elijah could have cared less about what I was feeling. That is what hurt the most. It's like he thought I wasn't deserving. So, I began to believe it too.

After the long, loving embrace from his wife, Eddie regained his focus on the crowd and said, "I want to say thank you to everyone for allowing me to talk to you tonight. Please, don't be afraid to seek help. Don't wait because the time is now. And tomorrow may never come. God did not give you this life to waste it. Learn to live it, learn to survive. Thank you."

As he waved to the audience, he led his wife back to their seats. This time, instead of hand claps, Eddie was offered 'God bless yous' and 'thank Gods' by the people. Just as I looked over at Annette, she looked over at me.

"That was deep, huh?" I asked.

"Yes, Deany. Indeed it was. I am still tearing up inside. I hope to God that I can find someone to love me like that someday."

"Yeah… me too."

Annette looked at me as I looked down. With sad eyes, she rubbed me on my back.

Pastor Benson once again stood at the podium. "Brotha Eddie, thank you for sharing your story. PTSD is a very serious condition that if left untreated could be very, very dangerous. May God continue to bless and keep you and your beautiful wife."

"Thank you, Sir." Eddie nodded as he massaged his wife's shoulders.

"Would anyone else like to share any thoughts tonight?"

Silence. You could almost hear folks breathing it was so quiet for that split moment.

"I would like to say something." The woman's voice was so inaudible that we could barely hear her. The audience began to look around and Pastor Benson leaned back into the podium.

"Who said that?"

"I did." It was Sista Patrice. The look on her face had such fear that she didn't make any eye contact with anyone. Sista Patrice stood up from her seat and just stood there. "If it's okay, may I just stand here?"

"Of course you may. Whatever makes you feel comfortable." Dr. J.J.'s attention was awakened just like everyone else's. It must be that 'doctor' in her because she was almost staring at Sista Patrice way more attentively than with Eddie.

"Hi… umm… everyone." She said without looking up.

"Hello," the voices echoed.

"My name is Patrice. I've been coming here for several weeks. You know… just to observe. I don't really know why I stood up or what I want to say, so, I guess I will just start." She grinned nervously then began to wring her hands together.

Annette leaned over and said, "She is about to have a nervous breakdown right in front of us."

"I think you are right, Annette," as she was beginning to make me nervous. I almost felt anxiety coming onto me through her. It was like I am feeling the exact physical fear that she is. Strange. I don't know this woman, but I feel her for some reason.

"You know, I really feel like I have seen her before," Annette whispered as she sat back up to listen to Sista Patrice talk.

Patrice began speaking. "Ummm.... well... I am not from here. I live about thirty minutes away in Jessupville. I've lived there all of my life. Being from a small town like that, where everybody knows everybody, can get very tough sometimes. Reason being is because everyone is always in your business. And I like minding mine."

A lot of 'umm-hmmms' and 'that's right" were being said.

"I have been really struggling the last few months because of a loss of a loved one. Well, I say loss because I haven't heard from him in months. Someone that I loved since college. I met him during my senior year. He was a very compassionate man that always saw my needs first. We were so young and full of life. But when it was time for me to graduate, he had another year to continue. I moved back here, found a job and really began to take off in my career. The distance was too much for both of us, so we went our separate ways. It was a very hard time. But we knew we would not have been able to continue our relationship being so far away."

The room was so still. Everyone was so attentive and mystified as to where Sista Patrice was going with her story.

"I found out that he was dating someone else and I was furious. Not sure why I was mad because it was initially my idea that we should break up. But anyway, I was mad at him for finding someone else and I just stopped all communication. I know I should not have been mad, because deep down inside, I wished he would have come for me. You know... like a *'knight in shining armor'*. It was silly, I know. But I was young and naive. And guess what? He never came." Patrice had a nervous grin that quickly faded.

"Somehow, after a few years, he was able to locate me. I guess with technology on the rise, finding people was much easier than back in the day. It was like a dream come true. After all of those years, he came back into my life. We could only spend weekends together because of his job. And I was okay with that. A little bit of time was better than no time. He moved to another part of town because of his work with the government. He worked as a contractor and it required him to randomly move about, so he could not settle down with me. He said he didn't want to marry me because he didn't want to put my life on hold or to put me in danger because of his work."

Annette leaned over again whispering, "Is she serious? Sounds like a 'playa' move." I motioned for Annette to stop whispering so loudly.

"When I became pregnant, we were both excited about the new addition we were going to have. But, I .... um," Sista Patrice sniffed. "I miscarried."

The room was very empathetic towards Patrice. Losing a child is an event that I can't even imagine.

"We were truly devastated because we both wanted that child. He knew how much it affected me emotionally. And for the last fifteen years, for every Mother's Day, he always brought me a Mother's Day gift." Sista Patrice's eyes lit up as she told the story. She even managed to smile as if it really was happening. "It was always in a small, pink gift bag."

Pink gift bag? The pit of my stomach just clenched so tightly that I thought I would vomit. But there is no way she could be talking about Elijah. No… no way. Now Patrice has my undivided attention. No one else's existence was in the room except me and her.

"It was never anything big inside the bag. It was just him acknowledging the fact that I was supposed to be a Mother. That was so special to me." Sista Patrice paused and tears welled up. We all sat there, not really sure what to say.

Before I realized it, I looked directly at Patrice and asked very boldly, "What was his name?" Puzzled, Sista Patrice took a moment and looked at me, stunned that I would ask that question. Annette whipped her head around at me too… surprised. Now, everybody's eyes were on me.

"His name?" The look of *'why is that your business'* came upon Sista Patrice's face, but she lifted her head up proudly and said, "Cornelius. Cornelius Montgomery."

CHAPTER FOURTEEN

"Say wha-a-a-a? What did you say?" The room started spinning. I think my heart stopped. I stood up from my seat and clenched my chest. I could feel the eyes of the other guest on me ... but I didn't care. The room began to spin a little faster... almost topsy-turvy. I think I am going to pass out. "Dear God, that can't be," I thought as I gazed at the woman who just admitted to loving my deceased husband. But wait... not only love him but conceived a child as well. He was cheating on me all of these years. My mind was spiralling at top speed.

Annette stood up and grabbed me by both arms. "Deany!" Now Annette was in full panic mode because my eyes were fixed on Sista Patrice like a wild woman and I was shaking uncontrollably. She shook me and yelled again, "Deany, what's wrong?"

By now, the shock has become rage. "Did you say Cornelius Montgomery? As in Elijah Cornelius Montgomery?"

"Y-y-yes." Sista Patrice stuttered and managed to frown at how nosy her church Sista was. "Why is that any of your business?" Sista Patrice snapped at me.

"You mean to tell me, over the last 16 years, my husband has been having an affair with you? And you are going to ask me why is that my business?" as I took a step towards Patrice's direction.

"Husband?" asked Annette. While looking confused, she kept questioning what just happened over and over in her head... not really understanding what she just heard. All the while still holding on to my arm.

"That sorry..." the look of disgust came over me and I rolled my eyes so hard, I thought they would get stuck behind my eye socket. "He betrayed my love and trust and made me feel like I was worthless for years," as I took another step. "He left me and my son at home while he came to see you?" And you question me as to why is that my business?" I was so mad, the hell in the inside of me dried up my tears. "It is my business Patrice because I was Elijah's wife!"

"Was? What do you mean was?"

"Was. Past tense. He is dead." I said with no emotion and no compassion.

I was in such a state of delusion, I didn't know Dr. J.J. had stepped in front of me to stop me from getting any closer to Sista Patrice. Pastor Benson moved beside Sista Patrice, just in case I got close enough to take a swing at her. By this time, the entire room was standing at their seats, in disbelief about what they just heard.

"Your dearly beloved has been dead for months now," I said sarcastically. "That's why you haven't heard from him. If you've been looking for Cornelius, you were using a middle name that he rarely used."

By this time, Sista Patrice was disheveled. "He's dead?" Pastor Benson grabbed her arm as she sat down on the chair. Looking up at me she said, "I never knew he was married? I swear." Tears rolled down on each cheek. "He never said anything about having a family… a son… or a wife. I'm sorry… I didn't know? Oh God…. I'm sorry." Sista Patrice collapsed in the arms of Pastor Benson. She wept. Not sure if she was upset because she just found out she was the other woman or the fact that Elijah was dead.

"Oh, my God!" Annette mumbled as she sat down in the chair next to where I was standing. "I remember," she gasped. Looking up at me, Annette motioned for me to sit down beside her. "Deany, I remember where I saw that lady from."

"Excuse me?"

"Remember when she first came in, I said I felt like I have seen her before? Well… I remember now." Annette put her head down and sighed. "Deany, I saw Elijah with this woman a few years ago and I didn't say anything?"

I pulled away from Annette in sheer disbelief and disgust. "You saw my husband with another woman and didn't say anything to me? You knew?"

"Judean, I'm sorry. You know I don't get in no one's business, so that's why …"

I stood up and grabbed my purse. I can't hear any more of this. As I turned to walk towards the door, Dr. J.J. tried to stop me.

"Judean, I know you are upset. This has been a lot to take in in this short amount of time. Can we please go sit down to talk before you leave?" Dr. J.J. asked.

I whispered, "No."

It felt like I was walking through sludge. I couldn't get my feet to move out of there fast enough. I heard Pastor Benson calling my name, but I just couldn't answer him. My head hurts. My heart is beating so hard, I'm sure the middle of my chest will have bruises later. I feel... dead. I might as well be. I died all over again back there. I ran across the road, not even looking for cars coming. In the back of my mind, maybe it would have been better if I had gotten hit. That way, I wouldn't feel anything anymore.

I cranked up my car and drove. No music. Windows up. That was all the solitude I needed. As I drove, I cried... I screamed ... I asked God, "Why me?" The man I loved obviously didn't love or want me. I was used and emotionally tormented. If he didn't want me, why stay with me?

My fists hit the steering wheel repeatedly. "I hate you, Elijah! I hate you! I hope you are burning in hell!" I screamed. And then, I thought about Annette. After all the years of so-called friendship, I believed in her. I tried to trust her. And she kept something from me that could have really changed the course of this entire situation. How dare she acted like she cared? I would have told her if her man was creeping. If she had one.

My mind ran back to all those years. All of the weekends Elijah left for work on Fridays to return on Mondays. The days he would leave for hours not accounted for, just assuring me he will be back later. And I never questioned him. What a fool I was. I was really simple to think or even admit that I truly trusted him. And for what? An affair that lasted almost half of our marriage.

"I'm so stupid!" I yelled. The tears are clouding my vision. I cried like a newborn baby. "God, I hate my life! I don't want to live like this anymore. I don't want to hurt. I don't want to feel unloved. I don't want to feel anything. I'm tired!"

A thunderous bolt of light flashed before my eyes… and everything was quiet.

CHAPTER FIFTEEN

What a beautiful day! So peaceful and quiet. I was walking in a field of long, green blades of grass. It was the greenest grass I had ever seen. Colorful butterflies were everywhere. The sun on my face was perfectly warm and soothing, but not hot. Looking up, I noticed the sky was so blue, it looked never-ending. What peace I feel. My mind was free from thought. No emotions were within me except happiness. What a joyful feeling to have. In a faint distance, I can hear the music. A beautiful array of melodies I've never heard before. There were instruments playing that I couldn't name. I don't care. It sounds amazing whatever it is. I love it!

A nagging feeling of discomfort was in my chest but the scenery I was viewing was a perfect distraction. I closed my eyes and stood still to absorb the feeling of tranquility.

"Judean." That voice sounded angelic. My eyes still closed, I waited for it to call my name again.

"Judean." My body jolted because this time, I recognized the voice.

"Momma Jean?"

I turned around to see Momma Jean standing before me. She was wearing a gorgeous white gown that seemed to glow. And she, she looked so young and beautiful. Before I realized it, I jumped into her arms, burying my head into her shoulders. I didn't want to let go. "Momma Jean! I missed you so much. I am so happy to see you, Momma Jean." When I let go to look at her, I touched my chest because that nagging feeling wouldn't go away.

"Judean, my beautiful girl." Momma Jean smiled. "I been prayin' Gawd's grace and mercy upon ya, child." Momma Jean's expression softens just a little for me to notice she had more to say.

"Shuga, as much as I love ya being with me, it's not ya time yet."

"Time? What do you mean not my time yet?"

"Judean, ya work for tha Lawd ain't over. Ya gots to go back and live tha rest of ya life. I knows it may not seem like it, but ya goin' through things for a reason, child. Even tho it seemed like Gawd was not there, He was always by ya side… even through ya hardest time."

A sharp pain pierced through my chest so hard, I bent over.

"NO! I don't want to go back, Momma Jean. I want to stay here with you. I finally feel at peace. All of my heartaches are gone." I knelt down and pleaded to stay.

"Judean, baby… that's why ya heart is hurting. Those doctors are trying everything in their power to bring ya back to life."

Inside Of Me

Another sharp pain, this time bringing tears to my eyes. "No, Momma Jean… please let me stay. I don't want to go back. There's nothing back there for me."

Momma Jean looked at me and smiled. "Ya 'life' is waiting on ya to come back, Shuga. My great-grandson needs his Momma." Momma Jean smiled so proudly. "Ya done a great job with that boy, Judean. Ya can't leave him just yet." Momma Jean knelt down and hugged me and said, "I loves ya, henh! But Gawd loves ya more!" Momma Jean kissed my forehead.

CLEAR

The electricity ripped through my body like a double-edged knife. I gasped life back into my lungs. I heard the doctors say, "She's back. Let's take her up to ICU and monitor her for the next few hours."

And just like that… I came back.

CHAPTER SIXTEEN

I hear sniffling. I feel someone holding my left hand. It's a man's hand - strong yet comforting. The sound of that beep… It's in sync with my heartbeat. Ummm… is that MY heartbeat? I'm trying to open my eyes. Oh, my head hurts. I hear someone. Who is that sniffling? Why can't I move? Dear God, why didn't you let me stay with Momma Jean? Wait… I saw Momma Jean! She wouldn't let me stay with her. She said I still had work to do. Work? That I still had something to live for; her great-grandson. (Gasp) Oh my God! EJ, my baby. I know he is worried about me. I wonder if he is holding my hand? EJ? Can you hear me? Sigh… I'm tired and sleepy. Maybe I can try to open my eyes later.

"Momma?" I heard EJ calling my name.

"Huh?" I mumbled. I was barely able to open my eyes to see EJ and Pastor Benson looking at me. I closed my eyes, thinking that I was dreaming.

"Momma!" EJ called my name a little more sternly. This time, he rubbed my arm to stimulate me.

"Yes, baby. I hear you."

"Sista Judean? Can you wake up for us?" Pastor Benson is really here.

"Pastor? I thought I was dreaming." I looked over and saw EJ looking at me. "EJ? Hey son." I was groggy and struggling to wake up, but I managed to smile.

"Blessed be thy name. Jehovah Rapha, you are a healer. Glory to your name, Jesus! Sista Judean, how are you feeling?" Pastor showed genuine concern in his eyes.

"I don't know. How did I get here? What happened?"

"You don't remember, Ma?" EJ was staring at me like I had died and resurrected on the third day.

"I remember…" I looked away from both Pastor and EJ. "I remember driving away from the group session." Still nervously looking away not wanting to meet the Pastor's eyes. "I remember I was upset."

"Do you remember why you were upset?" asked Pastor.

"Yes," I closed my eyes. "I remember."

EJ was puzzled. He looked at me, then at Pastor. "Can someone tell me what happened?"

"Not now, son. Please, not now."

EJ squeezed my hand tighter. "Okay, Ma. Don't get upset. I'm just glad you are here with me." The unconditional love I felt from that boy… I mean that man … is indescribable.

"What I don't remember is how I got here."

"Momma, you hit a guardrail going down highway 69."

"God's Angels of Mercy were covering you, Judean." Pastor said. "Your car should have flipped over. But the mighty hands of Jesus stopped you from going over the embankment."

"Momma ... did you intentionally try to hurt yourself?"

"W-w-what?" This time, I managed to sit up more just so I could get a good enough understanding of where EJ was going with his question. "Did I intentionally try to kill myself? Is that what you are asking me, EJ?" The frown on my bruised face really hurt, but it didn't hurt as much as the question that my son asked me. "Of course not!" I thought to myself, *did I?*

Just then, the doctor came into the room and was excited to see what I was awake. "Mrs. Montgomery, you had us really scared a few hours ago."

"A few hours? It's only been a few hours?" It felt like days have gone by. "What time is it?"

He looked that the wall clock behind me and said, "It is 3:14 a.m. And my name is Dr. Riggins, by the way. I am the trauma physician that worked on you when you came into the ER. This is not my floor. I only came up to see how my late-night patient was doing."

"This is not your floor? What floor am I on?"

EJ and Pastor looked at each other as the Doctor looked at them. "Mrs. Montgomery, after you stabilized in ICU, you were moved to the 7th floor of the Psychiatric Ward.

"Say what??? The Psych Ward? I'm not crazy!" I tried to get out of bed, but I felt a sharp pain in my chest ... almost a burning sensation.

"Mrs. Montgomery, it's okay. Try not to be alarmed," as Dr. Riggins tried to calm me down by rubbing my shoulder. "It's just a formality. You came through the ER saying things out of the ordinary - along with vehicular signs that you may have tried to harm yourself - so it was best to put you up here. Just for observation, of course. You will have to stay here for at least 72 hours. Which is a good idea, considering you bumped your head and you had to be revived on the scene because your heart stopped."

"My heart stopped?"

"Yes… twice." But thank God, you were brought back by the EMTs that assisted you." Dr. Riggins smiled at Pastor as if to get approval.

"My God!" Pastor looked up towards heaven. EJ still looked at me with great sadness in his eyes. It was at that moment he realized that his Momma died twice.

"However, I believe you are going to make a wonderful recovery. No broken bones, no serious trauma to your body, no imminent scarring … you are one lucky woman."

"Sista Judean, you are a BLESSED woman to come out of this alive. I give all honor and glory to God. You are still here on this earth for a reason and only God knows why. Your work is not done!" Pastor Benson exclaimed.

I looked at Pastor with wide eyes. Momma Jean said that very same thing to me. I don't know why. I am no one special. And I don't know what 'work' I can possibly do to make a difference.

Dr. Riggins said, "The nurse will be in throughout your stay here to take vitals, give you fluids and if you are in any pain, please let them know. Have a good morning. I will stop by later to check you." He nodded his head at Pastor and EJ and disappeared into the halls.

"Sista Judean, EJ, I'm going to grab a cup of coffee. EJ, would you like something?"

"No thank you, sir."

"Alright then. You two talk, I'll be back in a little while."

Pastor made his way out of the room and closed the door behind him. I looked at EJ and that look of terror was still in his eyes.

"Son, I'm okay. Really. I know it probably scared you and I am sorry. But I am alright."

"Momma… be honest with me. You have been going through so much over the years. And obviously, something upset you last night. Did you try to kill yourself?"

"No son, I did not."

"Momma, what happened last night that caused you distress? Please tell me. I won't be able to rest until you do."

My mind drifted back into that evening. That horrible evening where what little life I had in me was destroyed. I had no more emotion left. I couldn't cry. I won't cry - not anymore. I'm tired and I have given up on trying to understand my life. It is what it is. No one cares about me except EJ. No one has ever cared about me except Momma Jean and EJ. And now... who's left? Momma Jean has gone to be with the Lord and EJ is a grown man who is about to start his own life. So, who cares, right? I told EJ to pull up a chair to sit with me. I mustered enough energy to tell him about the 'confession' of Sista Patrice and Auntie Annette who knew about the affair and didn't say anything.

EJ's eyes were bloodshot. I could see the anger boiling through his veins.

"Son listen to me. I can understand how hurtful this must be to you. And I truly understand. But like I told you before, this is MY cross to bear, not yours. Elijah is and always will be your father. No matter what kind of man he was to me or what you may think of him now, he is still your father. You must try to let this go... for me? Please? I don't want you to suffer because of my despair over something that doesn't have anything to do with you." Lifting his chin up with my bandaged hand, I needed reassurance and asked, "Do you understand?"

"Yes Ma, I understand. I don't like it, but I respect your wishes. I love you, Momma! Please don't ever question my love for you!"

"Son, if I don't know anything else in this life, I know you love me! Now come here and give Momma a hug!"

CHAPTER SEVENTEEN

I reached for the remote and pressed the call button for the nurse.

"Yes, may I help you?" the lady in the intercom asked.

"Yes, please. Can I get something for my headache?"

"Sure thing. The nurse will be in in a moment."

"Thank you." Not sure if she heard my thank you since the intercom was quickly turned off. Laying in a fetal position, I looked out of the hospital window. It was a gloomy morning... just like my mood. The sky was gray, and the sun wasn't shining. I thought about EJ and his question to me. Did I try to kill myself? To be honest with myself, I really don't know. I can't remember the impact. I barely remember being in the car. As I thought back to last night, I began to feel sick to my stomach. A wave of nausea came across me something fierce. I sat up and looked around. Thank God I found a small wash bucket on my side table.

I vomited.

As I finished spewing out my insides, the nurse walked in. "Mrs. Montgomery, are you nauseated?"

Looking at her like *'Lady, did you really just ask me that after I just threw up my left kidney?'* I politely mumbled, "Yes."

"Okay, dear, let's get you some nausea medication along with some Tylenol so you won't feel sick again. You jolted your head during the accident, so you may have a slight concussion, which could cause your nausea." She put on the gloves she grabbed from the box on the wall and took the bucket away from me.

After disposing the contents of the bucket, the nurse went to the computer near the door, came back over to scan the band on my arm and went into the hall to get the medication I needed. A concussion, huh? Maybe that's why my head is hurting so badly. I thought that maybe last night's events were causing the stress and discomfort. Now I know.

The nurse came in with a syringe and a cup of pills. "I'm going to give you the nausea medicine intravenously so that it will work faster. And here is the Tylenol for your headache. Would you like some ginger ale to settle your stomach?"

"Yes, please."

"Okay dear. You may get a little drowsy with the medication. So, you rest, okay? I'll be back later to check on you."

And with that, the nurse left. Thank goodness. I am not in the mood to talk and surely don't want to listen to anyone. The nurse said 'rest'. And that I shall do. I am mentally exhausted and my body hurts. If I could just sleep so that I don't feel anything. Just sleep.

***

"Mrs. Montgomery?" I hear a woman who almost sang my name. It was sweet. As I opened my eyes, I see a fairly young, dark-haired woman standing over me. I wasn't startled because she almost looked like an angel. "Mrs. Montgomery, my name is Dr. Carlita, a psychiatrist here at the hospital."

"Oh, hi." I was preparing to sit myself up and she motioned for me to stop.

"No, Mrs. Montgomery. Please don't sit up. You need to relax and let your body rest, so you can get well faster. I just came by to introduce myself and to speak with you about our process. I understand you had an accident earlier this morning, correct?"

"Yes."

"I also understand that you had a very emotional night before the accident. The ER staff informed me of some of the things you said while being semi-conscious. That is why you are here. This is considered a suicide watch. Do you understand?"

"Yes. But I didn't try to end my life." I think my eyes shifted. She looked at me intently and I felt like if I made a sudden move, she would think I was lying.

Dr. Carlita smiled at me and said, "As part of your stay, you and I will have a session on tomorrow to 'talk'. We can talk about anything. As with any health professional, what we discuss will be strictly confidential. Once we conclude our session, I will let you know my opinion about the rest of your stay. Does that sound good to you?"

"I suppose."

"Why the frown, Mrs. Montgomery?"

"I guess I don't know what to expect. I've never actually talked to anyone about my problems until recently… with my son and my Pastor."

"Well Mrs. Montgomery, I can assure you that I am not here to judge or condemn you. I am here to listen. I will also assess your condition and help provide solutions, if I could, to help you adjust to dealing with life. Does that sound like something we can work on together?"

"Yes, and I appreciate your honesty. That actually makes me feel more comfortable. I appreciate your candor." I smiled at Dr. Carlita. She had such a sweet innocence about her.

"Great. I will see you tomorrow mid-morning. Please get some rest and have a great evening."

"Thank you. Good-bye."

As Dr. Carlita exited, I couldn't help but have a good feeling in my spirit about her. She seemed genuinely concerned. Not in a doctor-patient kind of way. But in a spiritual way. Thank you, Lord. I could use some positivity in my life.

***

I spent the entire day relaxing. I feel relieved that I don't have to think about anything. Not the accident, not Elijah, not Sista Patrice, not Annette… Annette. I felt a frown come over my face. I had forgotten all about her. She didn't come by nor call to see how I was doing. Not even to see if I was dead. Yeah… some friend. Of course, why should I be surprised? Sigh. I'm not surprised. Obviously, I was not ever important to her. I was a fool for even trusting her again since college. But hey…. screw it.

A different nurse was in today. She was a very nice, but a matter-of-fact woman. No time for the small talk… all business. Fine with me. I didn't feel like talking anyway.

The day was long but overall good. EJ visited me. He brought me a beautiful arrangement of colorful tulips and baby's breath. He also handed me a 'get well' and 'I love you' balloon. It was a beautiful addition to that ugly hospital room. It made my mood even brighter. Having him in my presence was truly a blessing. He never mentioned anything about my accident or why it happened. He looked relieved to know that he didn't lose me. He's even making plans to stay out a semester of school. "Absolutely not!" was my response. Of course, EJ can be as stubborn as his father, but there is no way I will allow that. I'm sure my answer went in one ear and out of the other, but time will tell if that happens. It also made me wonder, what would have happened to my son if I did perish? He may have thought that I actually did succeed in killing myself. That saddened my spirit. It never even occurred to me how much he may have suffered if I had died.

EJ left to go home. I'm glad he is staying at the house. It gives him some quiet time to study for his exams. The nurse came in and said I was strong enough to stand up unassisted and take a shower. I took her up on that offer. I guess being on this ward has its perks. A private room with a shower is what I needed. But to be on the safe side, I requested a shower stool just in case I suddenly feel weak.

I really felt unclean and wanted to wash the last few days off my body. As I stood under the water, I could feel the weight being washed away. I could literally feel what little cares I had dissolved. I felt good. Still sore and bruised, but good. I put on fresh underwear that EJ brought for me and I was able to put on my own pajamas. No sooner had I climbed back into bed, there was a knock at the door.

"Come in."

Pastor Benson walked in ... tall, distinguished, fine ... with a plant and a card. "Sista Judean, you are looking well, dear."

"Thank you, Pastor. I feel better."

"God is good all the time, Sista." He smiled and leaned over to give me a hug after he placed my gifts on the table. My God, he smells good.

"And all the time, God is good!" I responded.

"How are you feeling?"

"I am doing okay, Pastor. I mean, Phillip." We exchanged smiles. "I'm still sore, as to be expected. But good. Lord knows it could have been a different outcome." I looked at my plant from Pastor. Wow... it really could have been different.

"Praise be to God, Judean." Pastor looked around and found a chair in the corner. He pulled it up next to my bed. "I've had quite a number of calls asking about you. Church members and members of the depression group. The news seemed to have traveled rather quickly."

"Bad news travels fast. I can only imagine the discussion folks are having about me," I said sarcastically with a hint of pettiness.

"Well Judean, we can only ask God to keep YOU in perfect peace and let other folks talk. What they say behind your back is their business. It's nothing to concern yourself with. People talk. If they want to know the truth, they need to ask you. I've had several folks to ask what happened. And my response was 'only God knows' and I proceed to ask them what's going on in their lives." I snickered as Pastor peered over his glasses. "Having people talk about themselves sometimes catches them off guard. Their lives are not as exciting as someone else's."

"Amen to that, Pastor!" We both laughed. It was good to laugh. As sore as I was, laughing seemed like the best thing ever. Pastor Benson stayed for a long time and we talked about life in general. He was happy that EJ had some peace knowing that his mom was going to be fine. And the great thing about Pastor's visit? He never pressured me to talk about my past or that horrible night. We just ... talked.

CHAPTER EIGHTEEN

The next morning, I was kind of nervous about talking to Dr. Carlita. Not in a fearful kind of way. It was in an embarrassed way. Here I am, a middle-aged woman, still having issues with my past. Still hanging on to things that I can't seem to get rid of. Shouldn't I be past all of that by now? I should. I need to. Maybe I have become so complacent that I expect disappointment and failure. The only good thing that ever came out of my life was my son.

There was a knock on the door. Dr. Carlita was right on time. Unlike yesterday, Dr. Carlita doesn't look like a doctor. Today, she is wearing a pretty teal blue pantsuit which looks amazing with her dark hair. She was only carrying a notebook and pen. Her attire made me feel more comfortable… like we were girlfriends meeting up to talk.

"Good Morning, Mrs. Montgomery. How are you feeling today?"

"Good morning. Feeling refreshed. Much better than the last time you came by. And please, call me Judean."

"That is great news. And thank you, Judean." Dr. Carlita heard the nurse coming to the door. Opening the door, I saw the nurse bring in another sitting chair.

"Thank you, nurse."

"You are very welcomed, Dr. Carlita. Let me know if you need anything else while you are here."

"Will do." Dr. Carlita pulled the chair and placed it directly across from the other chair that was already in the room next to the window. "Judean, it is beautiful outside. I want us to sit next to the window while we talk. Is that okay?"

"Sure."

"If you need anything ... pillow, blanket ... bring it with you."

The room felt comfortable. It wasn't cold like you would expect in a hospital room. So, I just put on my hospital socks and walked to the chair. Dr. Carlita sat in the other chair across from me, opened her notebook and proceeded to write.

"Now Judean, I want you to relax. If at any time you need a break from our talk, please let me know. This is not meant to make you stressful or uncomfortable in any way, okay?"

"Okay."

"So, tell me about yourself? And you can start where ever you want to start."

For the last umpteen minutes, I told Dr. Carlita about my past. The good, the not-so-good, the bad and the ugly. This time, unlike my conversation with EJ, I didn't cry. I was all cried out. Numb and dead in the inside. I was an empty shell trying to maintain some sort of life. And this has been my life for a long time.

As I continued with my story, Dr. Carlita never changed facial expressions. She maintained the same composure as she did when she walked into the room... peaceful and pleasant. She kept eye contact and only wrote in her notebook when I paused in between stories. And she only interrupted me to ask questions just so she could get a better understanding.

Dr. Carlita was looking at me. I blanked out for a moment, thinking back to the days of 'what was'.

"Dr. Carlita, I have been in this state of depression for as long as I can remember. I can't remember any good days, except for when I had my son. Even then, I was a little unhappy. I had no help with the baby except Elijah whenever he wasn't meandering with other women. And yes, he was with other women. I knew it then. I was just naive and dumb and accepted it for what it was. I wanted a father for my child… our child. Also, my own Mother and sister didn't come to be with me when I had my first child. My sister was too busy living her life to think about coming to visit me. And my mom… well, I didn't expect her to come anyway."

"Why didn't you, Judean?"

"Because I wasn't my sister. She never cared about me as a child. It never changed when I became a woman. There was always an excuse why she couldn't come and see me. That's when I had to get a grip on reality and accept it for what it was. Nothing. It was a hard pill to swallow because every girl wants to feel loved by their mother. I never got that. That just wasn't meant for me.

"Judean, what kind of feelings do you have towards your mother?" Dr. Carlita stared at me not knowing what my reaction was going to be. In fact, I didn't need time to think. I didn't feel anything. It was as if my mother doesn't exist.

"Truthfully, I don't feel anything. How can I when I received absolutely nothing from her? Sure, I love her because she is my mother after all. But I don't have any emotional feelings. My feelings died when I was ten years old. And to tell you the truth, I don't feel bad about it. Maybe I should... but I don't. Dr. Carlita, for years, I longed for the love of my mother. Every daughter wants to feel that unconditional bond with the woman that gave birth to you."

This was the only time I felt misty, but crying was not an option - not today.

"If I am truly honest with myself, it was because of her that I never loved me. I felt like I was unworthy and not deserving. So, I never demanded that love from anyone, not even myself."

This is the first time that I have ever expressed - to anyone - the feelings that I have for my mother. I almost felt bad for even verbalizing what I have been feeling all of this time. How could I not have feelings for the woman who gave birth to me? But then again, how could she deprive me of the love I deserved? I was silent for a few minutes and Dr. Carlita started writing. The way she scribbled on that piece of paper was almost rhythmic.

"Judean, tell me about your depressive days? What did or do you feel like? How did or do you feel now? How did you maintain all these years with no help?"

I thought to myself for a moment. I literally had to really think, *how did I maintain?*

"Well... to be quite honest, I still don't know how I sustained my sanity. Depression feels like darkness... a hollow pit of darkness that no one or nothing can bring you out of. And it is so hard to get out. All I wanted to do was stay in bed with the curtains closed. No lights. No television. No nothing. Just complete silence. I didn't care if I ate. I didn't care if I showered. One minute I could be lost in my thoughts. The next minute, I am crying a river - and don't know why. I felt hopeless, incomplete, lifeless ... dead. I just didn't care about me at all. And neither did anyone else close to me. I know that there are people who have gone through so much worse than I have. But I felt like I was all alone to fend for myself."

I looked away as I began to think deep within. "There were so many dark days, so many times I felt like I was suffocating. It hurt to breathe. My body was an empty vessel. I even questioned God... *Why me?* What did I do to deserve all of the hurt I feel inside? When can I finally be happy? But all I heard was silence. And to me, no answer was an answer. The only thing that really got me out of my state for just a little while was EJ. When he was younger, I had to help him with his everyday needs. But as soon as he was done for the day, so was I. Elijah didn't understand. He didn't want to understand. He always made it a point to talk about not wanting to be involved with my 'pity party'. Imagine how I felt, knowing that my own husband never supported me. Never even cared about my well-being. It was during that time I knew I was really in this alone. That made me feel even more deserted. Frankly, Dr. Carlita, if it wasn't for my son... I really wouldn't even want to be here."

There, I said it. And I meant it. "So, in a nutshell, my son saved my life because HE was the only one worth living for."

I paused and smiled. Dr. Carlita starting her rhythmic writing again. This time, she wrote with an approving smile.

"I supposed that is why it was so hard for me when EJ went off to college. I was so proud of him and his wonderful accomplishments. He was accepted into the school he wanted to go to since middle school. But that day I had to leave EJ at his dorm, I felt like my heart was being ripped right out of my soul. The hurt of leaving my only child, my only means of survival, was devastating. I cried for days. No ... weeks. And Elijah... well, he thought I was overreacting. I probably was but still - no support from him. The love of a child is like no other. Each parent knows there will be a day when that child becomes an adult and must live their own lives. I just wasn't ready to let go. But I knew I had to. It has gotten better as the time goes by. As a young black man, living in these times, you worry a lot more now than during my time. All I can do is pray that

God keeps EJ safe from all the harm and danger this world has set out for him."

"I want to ask you something, Judean, and I want you to take a few minutes to think about this before you answer. Okay?

"Alright."

"What would make you happy?"

"Uh-h-h." Wow, did she catch me off guard with that question? "Dr. Carlita... ummmm... I've been unhappy for so long, I really don't know how to answer that question."

"Judean, I want you to understand something and I want you to hear me very carefully."

I was almost afraid of what Dr. Carlita was about to say. I guess my mind was preparing me for some sort of rant about 'you need to grow up' or 'you are too old for this' talk.

"You, Judean, are worthy of love. You are worthy of happiness in your life. You are a beautiful woman who has had a bad hand dealt to you at an early age. But that was the past; it's gone now. This is the present. You must take action RIGHT NOW to start living your best life. Do you understand what I am saying to you?"

A felt a knot like someone punched me in the throat. I couldn't help but look intently into Dr. Carlita's eyes. "Judean think about this. If you keep dwelling on what your mother, your sister, Annette, and Elijah did to you, you will never, ever be happy. And it is all because YOU won't let it go. You need to forgive all of the people in your life who have wronged you. And most importantly, you need to forgive yourself for allowing them to make you feel worthless. No one deserves the kind of mental abuse from anyone. You didn't deserve it. So, my question again, what would make you happy?"

Her words were electrifying. It jolted my body like I was hit with a taser. She was right. I had been holding on to this mess for so long, why haven't I let it go? Better yet, why haven't I moved on? I was so absorbed with the lack of love and support from the ones I loved, I lost myself... and never returned back.

"Well Dr. Carlita, I've always loved flowers. I'm actually pretty good with them. I've always imagined doing floral design as a hobby, but ..."

"No buts, Judean."

"Yes, I would like to pick up a hobby doing something I love." I smiled. She smiled and nodded.

"Anything else?"

"Honestly, I just want to be happy. I want to be around people who genuinely love me and want the best for me. I know it should be easy, but in my mind, it sounds like a hard task to accomplish."

"In the beginning, it will be hard because you've conditioned your mind to expect disappointments. You have no expectations for happiness. Tell me, how do you feel at this very moment?"

I felt warm and amazingly free. "I feel light and unbelievably happy. Even after finding out about my husband's infidelity, it's like I finally got the confirmation I needed to actually believe he was unfaithful. Originally, I was mad and hurt, but now I am relieved." I smiled so big, my cheeks hurt.

"I want to mention something to you before we end this session. I have a task for you to think about. I need for you to go to the people who have wronged you in the past and I want you to talk to them. Let them know exactly how you felt about the past and what you are feeling now. And before you end the conversation, I want you to forgive them. You don't have to do it the very minute you leave the hospital but in your own time. Can you think about it and decide on whether you are up to it?"

"Dr. Carlita, it's time. And you are right. In order for me to be happy, I need to let go. No matter how badly it may hurt, it needs to be done. But in my own time."

"Judean, I am proud of you. You are a remarkable person. Don't ever forget that and don't let anyone tell you differently, deal?"

"Deal!"

"Judean, just so you know, I am diagnosing you as clinically depressed but not suicidal. I believe at the time of your accident, you were distracted by the evening's events and wasn't paying attention. You don't display having a desire to end your life, which is great. However, I am going to prescribe an antidepressant for you to take for the next few months. You should be feeling better and being more active within two weeks. If you are having an episode and need to speak with someone, please call my office. Also, I will have the nurse to schedule appointments with you to see me over the next few months as well. With that being said, I will write up your discharge papers so you can go home within the next few hours. Do you have any questions for me?"

"No, I don't. Thank you for ... just thank you." I got up out of my chair and hugged Dr. Carlita. I hugged probably a little too tightly, but she didn't complain.

As Dr. Carlita left the room, I returned to the bed and just sat there thinking about what just happened. I have a chance to start living again. I closed my eyes and thanked God for saving a poor fool like me. *'Lord, thank you for sparing my life and giving me an opportunity to live a new chapter to my Book of Life. God, I am forever grateful. Thank you!'* As I opened my eyes, I jumped out of the bed to call EJ to come to pick me up from the hospital. I'm going home.

CHAPTER NINETEEN

As the weeks went by, I began to feel better and better. I have no thoughts about my past. I only think about what is in front of me. My 'right now'. Pastor Benson allowed me to be in charge of the floral arrangements in the church. And because of that, I started getting requests from church members to make arrangements for special occasions. God is good. It took a small passion to expand to a small business. For each floral arrangement I make, I always attach a wallet-sized card with a bible verse. The verses are always positive and inspirational. They are wallet-sized so that anytime someone may feel down or know someone that has been going through, they will have this card to look at or can pass it on to someone in need. Hey, I am not looking to make a lot of money. I just enjoy being needed and appreciated. And I also enjoy being able to make someone smile from something I created. It makes me …. happy. Maybe, this is what Momma Jean was talking about.

***

One afternoon as I was piecing together some flowers for an order, my mind ran on Dr. Carlita. She asked something of me in the hospital room and mentioned it a few times in our sessions. Closure. As I walked over to the window and looked out, I couldn't help but feel in my spirit *IT'S TIME*. Yes, it is time to start closing all of the partially open chapters in my life so that I can focus on the good one that is open now. My mother and I haven't spoken in a number of months. She is busy following behind her glory… my sister. But hey, if she likes it, I love it. Eventually, I will determine when I want to close their chapters. And I am okay with that. So, for now, I'm good with them. I walked over to my purse and pulled out my cell phone. Inhale. Exhale. I dialed.

"H-h-h-hello? Deany?" Annette answered the phone like I was the Ghost of Christmas Past.

"Hello, Annette."

"Deany, you caught me by surprise. I didn't expect you to call me. Listen, I've been meaning to …"

"Stop! Let's not start off this conversation with lies, okay?" I heard Annette gasp and she is not one to shut up easily. "You were not going to call me. If you were really concerned about me, you would have been there next to me in the hospital the night of my accident. But you weren't … were you?"

Awaiting her response, she finally said, "No. I wasn't. But Deany, I felt like I was the cause of the accident."

"Tell me, what made you feel that way?"

"Well, because of what went down that night. I told you that I saw Elijah with that woman. Deany, I'm really and truly …"

"Sorry? Annette, just stop. I didn't call to hear you make excuses to me. That is just a waste of time and I'll tell you why. You've never had my back... EVER. When you said you had seen Elijah and Sista Patrice together, but didn't say anything, I wasn't surprised. I understand now that it really wasn't your place to get in between married folks' business. However, you and I had known each other way before Elijah came into the picture. I assumed our sisterhood took precedence over a man. But I was wrong. And that was MY fault. With that being said Annette, I forgive you. I truly forgive you for everything."

After a long pause, Annette said, "Thank you, Judean."

"You, Annette, are welcomed." I truly hope she can sense the sincerity in my voice. She has no clue how ecstatic this makes me feel.

"I also thank you for life lessons about love, friendship, and humility. In my current journey through life, I have finally begun to realize that I deserve more than what this life has to offer. And I pray every day that I continue to have the peace I have now. Peace knowing that God alone loves me beyond any man or woman can love me. And that peace does not include you. Goodbye Annette. May God continue to bless you and I pray nothing by the best for you."

CLICK

And just like that, it was done. I stretched my arms out and twirled around like a seven-year-old child. "Yes!" It felt good to let part of the baggage go. Such a freeing feeling. I gathered my composure and went back to table to finish the flower order I had started.

***

As I got ready for bed that night, I thought about how it ended with Annette. Now I know how it feels to have dead weight lifted off. What an incredible feeling! I felt like I could breathe. I walked over to my bed and slipped under the covers, ready to slumber for the night. And then I thought about Momma and Elijah. How can I get their heavy weight off of me, too? Marjorie, well she was irrelevant at this point. She is my sister and that is about it. She is doing her, so I will do me.

I jumped out of the bed and opened my vanity where I kept my journal. Grabbing the book, I scrambled in the drawer for a pen, then I remembered I had one in my purse. As I collected my items, I went and sat on the bed. I propped myself up against the headboard and exhaled. This is it. This will complete my healing. I started thinking about what to say after all of this time. Carolyn… I will start with her. She was the very first person that was supposed to love me. She failed. It took me all of this time to realize that I can't make anyone love me, not even my Mother. And I can't allow her lack of love to ruin me forever. I took a deep breath and started writing.

Momma,

I sincerely pray this letter reaches you in good health. I know you are wondering why I am writing to you instead of calling? In the past, you have always seemed bothered whenever I want to have a serious conversation with you. And this seems like the best option for me… writing.

I have spent most of my childhood and a part of my adult life trying to receive some sort of approval from you. More than anything, I wanted and needed love. However, all of your love was given to Marjorie. Before you assume that I am jealous of the relationship you have with my sister, the truth is... I am! I am your daughter also. And I deserved my Mother to love me the same way Marjorie received love from you. But I never got it. And I have finally accepted the fact that I never will. Just know, at this point in my life, I am okay with that.

Momma, I will always love you. Despite what or how you feel about me, I always will. Also, I forgive you. I forgive you for making me feel worthless and unworthy. I forgive you for not loving me when, of all people, it was your love that I needed the most. I never thought that I would ever say this but THANK YOU! Thank you for giving me life. I finally know what it feels like to 'live'.

Take care of yourself, Carolyn. Best regards,

Judean

I looked at the letter I wrote and giggled to myself because I am not one to be petty. However, to see her reaction when she sees 'Carolyn' at the end of the letter would be priceless. After sealing the letter in an envelope, I knew it was time to deal with Elijah. Sleep was trying to overcome me, but this was too important to 'sleep on it'. I repositioned myself in the bed so I could focus more intently on my last thoughts for tonight.

***

The next morning, after I dropped off Carolyn's letter at the Post Office, I was at the cemetery at 8 am. I was wearing red... only because Elijah said I *'looked like I was gaining weight'* in that color. Today was my day and I was going to wear whatever I wanted to wear! I put on my red pumps too... and if it got dirty walking through this graveyard, so be it. I walked the path until I got to Elijah's grave. On top of his headstone was a bouquet of flowers. The card said, 'My love'. *I guess Sista Patrice found you after all*, I thought to myself. Then again, it could have been someone else. Who cares?

I stood over Elijah. I had no emotion to give other than a smile. It almost felt sinister, but it was a smile nonetheless. I looked around to make sure I was the only one there. That way, if I needed to talk loud enough for Elijah to hear me, I could. I chuckled. Get yourself together Judean. This is serious. I unfolded the piece of paper I was writing on last night and proceeded to talk to Elijah.

Dear Elijah,

I am here today to tell you how much I despised being with you. I was so young and dumb, but I loved you. You can't help who you love, right? Well, in my stupidity, I chose you. (haha)

Giggling like a schoolgirl, I looked around to make sure I was still there by myself. I continued.

But seriously... only one good thing came out of our union. It was our son, EJ. I want to say I hate you... but I won't. It was because of you and God

that I got the greatest gift that anyone could have ever given me. But everything else was pure hell. I never believed you loved me. You showed me that every time you were around me. You were too busy chasing other skirts rather than to be with your wife. At a time when I needed you the most, you were never there. You were a miserable, narcissistic man and I pray every day that your son never turns out to be like you.

Feeling a frown come over my face, I quickly regained my composure. Elijah has no hold over me anymore.

However, Elijah... I forgive you. I forgive you for all the wrong that you have done to me. I forgive you for all the infidelity. I forgive you for all the lies and the secrets you told me. I forgive you for all the tears I cried over you. I forgive you for not being the supportive husband that I needed in my life. I forgive you for everything. Because if I don't forgive you, God will not bless me with the life I deserve. I am happy. I am free. I am blessed to be able to start a new life... free from disappointments and negativity. And now that I have forgiven you, I can forgive myself.

I am excited about my new life. The one thing that I pray about is that God will send me a man who will love me, care for me, support me like a real man should. And He will send a man that I will least expect. I am speaking that into existence right now!! I proclaim the victory!!

I looked around... not caring this time. I yelled like my life depended on it.

Elijah... I am done with you. Good-bye forever!

And with that... I took a lighter out of my pocket, lit the end of that letter and watched it burn as I placed it on top of his grave. All of the hurt, pain, resentment, anger, hate ... it all went up in flames. As the little pieces of ash floated in the air, so did my peace.

"THANK YOU, JESUS - I AM FREE!" I shouted to the sky.

What an amazing feeling of peace like no other. Looking up towards the sky, I exclaimed jokingly as I walked down the path to my car, "Now Lord, if you could just send me that man I was talking about, my day would be complete!" I smiled to myself as the warm sun began to get just a little hotter.

Just then, the cell phone in my pocket buzzed. Looking at my phone, I stopped in my tracks. I felt my eyes get wide and my knees buckled. I stuttered. "H-h-hello?"

"Hello, Judean. I was thinking about you and decided to give you a call."

"Hello, Pastor... I-I-I mean, Philip."

ANXIETY AND DEPRESSION ASSOCIATION OF AMERICA

Founded in 1979, ADAA is an international nonprofit membership organization dedicated to the prevention, treatment, and cure of anxiety, depression, OCD, PTSD, and co-occurring disorders through education, practice, and research.

ADAA's unique interlinked consumer and professional mission focuses on improving quality of life for those with these disorders.

https://adaa.org

8701 Georgia Avenue
Suite #412
Silver Spring, MD 20910
Phone: 240-485-1001
Fax: 240-485-1035

Families for Depression Awareness

Families for Depression Awareness helps families recognize and cope with depression and bipolar disorder to get people well and prevent suicides.

http://www.familyaware.org

391 Totten Pond Road, Suite 101
Waltham, MA 02451
Telephone (781) 890-0220
Main office (615) 345-0420

Satellite office in Nashville, TN
Fax (781) 890-2411

Email info@familyaware.org

www.ingramcontent.com/pod-product-compliance
Lightning Source LLC
Chambersburg PA
CBHW071404290426
44108CB00014B/1680